JUMBO T

CW00969365

DOMINIC PRINCE is a freelance journalist and documentary maker who writes in the *Telegraph*, *Sunday Times*, *Daily Mail*, *Mail on Sunday*, *Independant on Sunday* and *The Racing Post*. He has made numerous films about horses including on Lester Piggott, a bloodstock agent and a rag and bone man. He is married to the food writer Rose Prince, and lives in London, currently on a diet of lentil broth and oatmeal.

DOMINIC PRINCE

Jumbo to Jockey

One midlife crisis, a horse
and the diet of a lifetime

FOURTH ESTATE • *London*

First published in Great Britain in 2011 by
Fourth Estate
An imprint of HarperCollins*Publishers*
77–85 Fulham Palace Road,
London W6 8JB
www.4thestate.co.uk

LOVE THIS BOOK? WWW.BOOKARMY.COM

Copyright © Dominic Prince 2011

1

The right of Dominic Prince to be identified as the author
of this work has been asserted by him in accordance
with the Copyright, Design and Patents Act 1988

A catalogue record for this book is
available from the British Library

ISBN 978-0-00-728867-0

All rights reserved. No part of this publication may be
reproduced, transmitted, or stored in a retrieval system,
in any form or by any means, without permission
in writing from Fourth Estate.

Typeset in Minion by G&M Designs Limited,
Raunds, Northamptonshire

Printed in Great Britain by Clays Ltd, St Ives plc

Mixed Sources
Product group from well-managed
forests and other controlled sources
www.fsc.org   Cert no. SW-COC-001806
© 1996 Forest Stewardship Council
FSC

FSC is a non-profit international organisation established to promote the
responsible management of the world's forests. Products carrying the FSC
label are independently certified to assure customers that they come
from forests that are managed to meet the social, economic and
ecological needs of present and future generations.

Find out more about HarperCollins and the environment at
www.harpercollins.co.uk/green

For Rose

PROLOGUE

It's early January and I am standing on the scales, singing. I come from a long line of people who sing out loud. My dad did it and my son Jack has inherited the trait. Not that I have much to sing about where I am standing now, mind. I can't see my feet and it is only by peering over the expanse of my stomach that I can see, aged forty-seven, I am topping 16½ stone. While it was not always like this, it is not entirely surprising. I was born at the beginning of January 1961 at what was then the London Hospital, Whitechapel, in the East End of London. I weighed in at 11lb 6oz and remained for the rest of the year the fattest baby born at the London Hospital. I find it difficult to believe that my mother has ever forgiven me.

My clothes are tight. The waistband on my trousers cuts into my paunch and the 16-inch collars pinch at my Adam's apple. The flesh rumples beneath the top button, and it feels like slow strangulation. I have been fighting an unwinnable battle for years, brought on by my own greed and slothfulness. Running for a bus is not nice. Little nodules erupt on the inside of my thighs and they are pretty painful. They are only there because my thighs are too fat and rub together like great elephant legs. I have a constant nagging paranoia about my health, high blood pressure and the possibility of a heart attack and a multitude of other life-threatening diagnoses, and yet I have hardly taken any exercise for two and a half decades.

I'm a middle-aged journalist, with a twenty-a-day fag habit. I drink much more wine than I should, and eat more than almost anyone I know. The prognosis is not ideal. My wife says she fears for the future. 'What, that I might die?' I ask, expecting her to break down in self-pitying tears at the prospect. 'No, that you might have a stroke aged fifty and I'll be lumbered with looking after you for the rest of my life.' She's nothing if not down to earth, my wife.

Although my condition is entirely self-inflicted, in my defence I must say that I do not stuff myself with junk food and drink gallons of lager. My girth has been built, not only on thousands of great restaurant lunches that were tradition-ally part and parcel of a hack's life, but on a delicious supply of home cooking. My wife, Rose, is a cookery author and food critic. For the last ten years she has written on a subject she is passionate about, and I have been happily sampling the by-product of her career. We both love eating and are obses-sive about buying good food, going to what most people would think extraordinary lengths to eat the best.

In our house in London we grow our own vegetables in old wooden wine boxes and at the cottage in Dorset we plant them in a raised bed in the garden. I make bread from the wonderful oily flour supplied by Mr Stoate from Shaftesbury who mills his wheat between two stones using the River Stirkel to power the milling process. We have even kept sheep. When we were first married we kept a variety called Castlemilk Moorit and more recently I bought eight Texel lambs that we fattened and had killed in our local slaughterhouse. We then feasted on the sweet, crisp-skinned and beautifully butchered animals.

Over the years we have travelled thousands of miles to seek out the most delicious, well-hung, black sides of beef from an array of butchers around the country. The best sausages that I have ever eaten come from John Robinson, a butcher in Stockbridge, Hampshire. Sausages are one of my top ten favourite meals. Mr Robinson sells three tons a week at his tiny shop, on a counter no more than 15 feet long, and he employs around eighteen butchers. The meat and game is exemplary. Every child in the world I have ever met goes mad for Stockbridge sausages, and fights have even broken out over them they're so good. They mince English shoulder of pork, add sage and other herbs and pump out the sausages by the trayful. They don't use preservatives, so they won't do mail order. If you want Robinson's sausages you have to go and collect them, but the journey is worth it.

A little further down the A30 from Stockbridge, going towards Salisbury, is Hollom Down Growers, a smallholding-cum-market garden where the most luscious soft fruit grows and ripens. In season, there are fields and fields full of huge, sweet strawberries, petite juicy raspberries, and tomatoes with such intense flavours that they might have been grown in Tuscany. Potatoes, leeks, apples, squashes, cucumbers, lettuces, peas, beans and onions can all be found there. And then there is always the creamy, sometimes sharp-flavoured cheeses assembled on the kitchen table for picking at and devouring after dinner in huge swathes of unadulterated, masticating passion.

Rose has always said that she has a terror of running out of food and, like me, she hates to miss a meal. She is sometimes recklessly extravagant when buying food and always buys too much. She does, however, love feeding people and having hordes of friends and family to dinner. On any given night, with our two children, we will eat a joint of well-hung and bloodied beef, then, the following day, we eat stacks of cold, rare roast beef sandwiches or bowls of spiced broth, made from the beef bones, with delicately cut strips of translucent, ruby meat.

Rose does the same with chicken. With the leftovers of a roast she will make a pot of rich stock from the simmered bones. She uses this to make sublime and creamy soups, sometimes with watercress, at other times with squash or celery leaves. Sometimes she scatters pieces of crisp smoked bacon over these soups, or crumbles a piece of fried black pudding, or adds an extra dash of cream. We will then eat the soup with the bread I have baked along with great glacier-sized chunks of melting unsalted butter.

More stock goes into the comforting risottos that we eat regularly, unctuous pools of slowly cooked rice scattered with Grana Padano cheese. Sometimes these will have added porcini or asparagus; sometimes they are simply seasoned with saffron or handfuls of chopped fresh herbs.

Without question, my favourite dish is game. In winter we can always look forward to enjoying dishes of pheasant, grouse and partridge with buttered baby turnips, carrots and spinach. We will eat them with fried breadcrumbs, bread sauce or sometimes roast them on a slice of bread. Potatoes come roasted in beef dripping or goose fat, or are sometimes mashed with hot milk and butter. If there are seconds I am first in the queue. Then there are the peripheral delicacies I love to pick at between meals. We both love cheese, and spend far too much on artisan cheddar, buttery blue cheeses or interesting little rounds of bloomy rinded cheeses made with ewes' milk.

Feeding children brings the inevitable opportunity to snack on their six o'clock leftovers – a nibble of bread-crumbed fish here, a mouthful of pasta there. Sometimes we will order a takeaway of a few deliciously buttery curries, popadoms, bhajis and chapattis, and when the children have had their fill I will put away anything that is left on the table.

But it is not just the food. For as long as I can remember I have drunk a lot of wine. Not every night but most evenings I will get through a bottle, perhaps a bit more. Although this is way above the recommended daily intake I do not seem to suffer ill-effects, apart from being too fat. There is no diabetes, few bad hangovers, no greater loss of concentration, in fact nothing that would serve as a warning that I am drinking too much and I rarely wake full of remorse, cursing the night before.

My exercise consists of walking to the newsagent for a newspaper and, if I am smoking, a packet of fags. Rose also takes up and gives up smoking intermittently, but regularly runs round our local park. The fitter she has become the more frequently she asks when I will try to do something about my weight, or take a break from drinking so much. I have always had a good line ready when under attack: 'I am putting a date in the diary,' I will say. 'After the wedding/birthday/dinner/Christmas party' – delete as appropriate. Exercise, if it is taken at all, has been both irregular and painful: the odd swim and game of tennis if the weather is nice. But both leave me feeling knackered and unable to move properly for days after. There was a game of football once with some friends in Battersea Park. We played against a group of young kids and after an hour we were so exhausted that we spent the rest of the afternoon in the pub and vowed never to play again.

My dad was forty-two when he was diagnosed with multiple sclerosis. As a young man he had been a smoker and drinker, but shortly after he became a father he gave up the fags, cut down on the booze, got fit and was enjoying life. When he was diagnosed he was in better shape than he had been as a teenager, but it was all too brief. When he was first diagnosed he spiralled into depression and retreated to bed to die. For six weeks he hardly moved, and in the end only got up when we stopped taking him food. He died nineteen years later.

Part of the reason why I have not stopped smoking or drinking is that neither of these things killed my dad. I have always possessed a nonsensical fear that if I follow his route to fitness and redemption the same fate might strike me. There was little logic to the reasoning, but it is a fact that the fitter you get the more you worry about your health. As a consequence, ever since I turned forty-two I have been waiting for some kind of diagnosis like the one given to my father. In the dark hours of my midlife crisis these are the thoughts that regularly haunt me.

While my brother was like my mum, I was always very much my father's child. We had the same mop of hair and were of a similar temperament, and perhaps it is because of this that, daily, I convince myself that I have some life-threatening illness. Sometimes it's knee cancer, sometimes throat, other times lung. I still remember when, aged eleven, I read in a Sunday supplement about a young girl who got cancer on the ball of her foot. I was convinced that was going to happen to me.

I was thirteen when my father was diagnosed, the same age my own son, Jack, is now, and it was around this time that the horse bug really took hold of me. It grabbed me by the throat:

there's nothing like the horse when you're feeling down. I'd had the experience before when I was much younger, when we lived in Muswell Hill and not grotty Ealing, where we subsequently moved to. While my father was being eaten by his horrible disease I sought solace with the horse. I would tiptoe out of the house and take the train to the stables in Harefield where we kept a series of ponies, first Bracken and then Gambol. The journey from our suburban house in Ealing, which I hated, took over an hour, and the closer I got to the stables the more I felt I had got away from the suffering at home. I used to get the train to Ruislip and then walk the three miles to the stables. Sometimes Mum would drive me but, as I know now, ferrying children around to something you are uninterested in can be particularly soul-destroying. I would stay there long after dark, until the stable owner was closing up and only then, reluctantly, walk back to the station and wait for the last train home. Mum would occasionally feign an interest in riding. Once or twice she even had a couple of lessons, but they were really only taken to placate me.

During those first years I would do anything to be surrounded by horses. There is something untouchable and unknowable about them, and they were as magical to me as characters in my favourite children's stories. When I was around them I was able to forget for a moment what was happening to my father. I loved stroking them, but I was just as happy watching them in the field, or observing them eat and drink.

It is now more than twenty years since I last rode a horse. We have two children. There are other distractions along with the duty of putting food on the table. But I have regrets, and the one I feel most keenly as I observe others who have been successful in one horse business or another is that, through a combination of fate and error, I never pursued that promised career in the equine world. More than that is the nagging reminder that *I have never done the one thing I have always wanted to do – competed on a horse in a race, on a racecourse.*

Since I was a teenager I have been drawn to horses, riding and the world of horse racing, but I have never ridden in any type of race. In those early years of hanging around ponies, drowning in their aroma, I never had the bottle, the skill or the bravery to put them, or myself, to the physical limits of both our capabilities. I competed in hunter trials and gymkhanas, and have a very old sackful of rosettes to prove it. I have a grand photo, too, of me and my dad in an equine fancy-dress competition. Dad is leading me on a white pony called, funnily enough, Prince. A tiny thing and perched on top of him is me in a fantastic outfit; I mean a really brilliant, clever outfit. I was dressed as a bottle of whisky and my dad held a banner aloft proclaiming 'You can take a White Horse anywhere', a play on the in vogue advert of the time for White Horse Scotch whisky. My mum had spent days designing and making the outfit. We won the show. Later on there was a bit of jumping, too, the higher the better, and even though my pony at the time, Bracken, was tiny, he would jump any obstacle put in his way. But as much fun as those riding days were, it was not quite the same as actually racing a horse. And this is what I have really always wanted to do.

There is one certainty about riding in a race and that is that you have to be a particular weight. A 16-stone man has never ridden in a horse race, let alone won one, even though I once suggested in the racing column I write for *The Tablet* that there should be horse races for fatties in which the jockeys have to have a minimum weight of 15 stone. In my daily, very urban life in London this is the closest I now get to living out my dream, and yet almost every day I am haunted by the lure of the horse. The pull remains infectious and the desire to ride returns time and again.

It was not just my weight and general listlessness that sparked the fire to get reunited with the animal I love most in the world. I have enjoyed a good living combining the worlds of journalism and television to follow what I love, but I am at a time in my life where I am feeling disappointed, somewhat unfulfilled. Middle age is upon me, and with it has come the crisis. I will not have many years left in which to fulfil a child-hood dream. Time, therefore, to do something extraordinary – just once.

One evening after Christmas, Rose and I were finishing a bottle of wine and having a 'big conversation' about our lives. The usual discussion about how we both drink too much (we do) and how we should cut down (which we also do from time to time) was interspersed with the reality of my weight and general lack of fitness. I weigh four stone more than I should and I am only five foot ten. 'If you won't lose weight for me what would you do it for?' she asked. And then the words came out of my mouth. I don't know why and I can only guess that I had been meaning to say them for a very long time. 'I'd lose weight to ride again.' Rose thought I meant hacking through woodlands or having a steady canter along verdant green turf or practising the forgotten art of the rising trot. I could see she was entirely unimpressed. And then I said: 'I'll do it to ride in a race, on a proper racehorse on one of Britain's racetracks.' That stopped her in her stride. She thought it was a great idea and from that moment onwards for the next ten months I put every effort into pulling it off.

Chapter One

The basic arithmetic was simple. To become a jockey I needed to lose five stone, to get under the minimum allowance of 12 stone. Having never been on a diet of any sort in my life before, I had no idea how long it would take or how to do it, apart from the obvious things of not eating or drinking too much. But I assumed, not unnaturally, that it would probably take a hell of a long time. If I could lose half a stone a month then by September I would have lost enough weight to be ready to race. But before I could establish when to race and how to diet, there was the question of how I could teach myself not to eat so much when surrounded by people who spend a good deal of time shopping and cooking mountains of food.

The first thing that had to be cut out was bread and pasta and butter and cheese. I remember my mother, who claimed constantly to be on a diet, saying years ago that she did the same thing. There was no precise science involved to suggest that this was the best way to proceed, but it felt like the right place to begin. The day after my announcement, Rose and I worked through what I might be able to eat and how it would fit in with what we would both still enjoy eating, since she had decided to take on the diet as well. It was not easy. We haggled and bickered and then discussed it all before reaching a compromise of sorts.

The conundrum of the diet was that since all athletes – footballers, boxers and rugby players among others – take a huge amount of carbohydrates on board, pasta and the like was a natural part of their daily intake. If I was going to be exercising for the first time in more than twenty years and put unfamiliar pressure on my body, carbohydrates would be essential for refuelling. But I wasn't an athlete and, besides, jockeys ate virtually nothing. Where was the middle ground? We decided that, rather than simply starve four stone off my body, we would start with a diet of pulses, beans, lentils – protein – lots of vegetables, salads and fruit, and wait and see what happened. The hardest part was the wine, which had been a part of my daily life since I got my first job, but that too was struck off the list, and then put back on, before being taken off again, and finally being allowed – in moderation.

Next on the list of things to do was to call everyone I knew in the horse world – trainers, owners, agents and managers – to find out what chance I had of riding a horse on a proper racecourse. No one took me seriously. Most people said it was a mad idea and that I would soon come to my senses. Others said that there was a good probability of me killing myself. The rest just howled with laughter. But then, when I said that I really was going to do it and that no one was going to stop me, the tone changed, and I started to get the advice I needed.

What was immediately apparent was that before I could go anywhere near a horse I needed to get fit and to lose a lot of weight. Until I had done that no one was going to let me ride. Quite apart from the fact that a Thoroughbred racehorse is a very delicate creature, the dangers of falling off one are exacerbated when you are overweight. The extra pounds make riding a horse a tricky balancing act, and if you do fall off with an extra four stone of ballast pushing down on you as you connect with the ground, broken bones are inevitable. I was told to watch footage of the greatest jockeys, men like Lester Piggott and Frankie Dettori, to see how their remarkable balance and rhythm did not upset the horse's natural gait. If the horse is put off its stride it will lose valuable ground. As I watched old tapes of their famous victories I clutched my girth and laughed to myself as I thought that this was what I was hoping, in my own way, to emulate. But I had to start somewhere.

If there was one real concern, though, it was that the pursuit of a childhood dream, in itself, was worryingly selfish, since this was all about the urge to pursue a dream that had been gnawing away at me for years. It would mean cutting myself off from my wife and children for weeks at a time as I disappeared to the countryside to train. It would mean a disruption, not just to our everyday diet but also to the children's wellbeing, and our family life. It left me with the nagging question that I should be have been concentrating on being a responsible father. Others who had faced a midlife crisis had just gone out and bought a Porsche. Why, some asked, couldn't I just go off and do that? On the other hand, I reasoned with myself, hadn't the children for years thought that they had a rather eccentric fat bloke for a father, who just ate too much? For as long as they could remember they only ever saw me with a glass of wine in my hand. Surely I could do better than that? This, then, would be a new era, a challenge the like of which I had not had for years, certainly not within their lifetime.

For as long as I can remember breakfast has usually consisted of a few slices of toast with marmalade, perhaps a fried egg or a couple of rashers of bacon. Occasionally I would have a Stockbridge sausage or two, all washed down with a mug of tea with full-fat milk. What I would now be presented with at the start of each day was a breakfast truly fit for a horse. Every evening I would prepare a meal of deliciously malted crushed barley, oats, linseed and a dessert spoon of honey all soaked overnight in water. It was a cold porridge-style gruel, which was not much to look at, but was far from unpleasant, and very early on it became the highlight of my day. This was supplemented by a strong cup of Earl Grey, with skimmed milk. Without doubt the best Earl Grey available is Fairtrade tea bags sold by the Co-op. It used to be that Safeways was the best but that particular enterprise folded into Morrisons and they foolishly did away with the tea. The breakfast felt healthy, and almost immediately I could feel the difference as I digested the food quickly, and it left me buzzing with a new energy. Within days I felt better than I had in years.

Whereas before lunch constituted grazing over delicious leftovers with a glass of wine (permanently topped up), it now became a meal consisting of salad with a piece of fish or cold chicken. White beans with olive oil, thyme and tuna was another favourite; it is so good that it has become a household speciality, with which I serve up pots of tiny brown Puy lentils with finely chopped celery, onions and carrots cooked for 20–25 minutes in chicken stock. To cook the lentils, first I fried the vegetables in olive oil, then added the lentils, stirring vigorously for 2–3 minutes and then finally the chicken stock. It was a warming, intense experience and it kept the bowels open. Dinner was taken after a walk with Billy, our dog, and would generally consist of more of the lentils cooked earlier in the day, a piece of steak and a salad.

To supplement these home-made concoctions I drank between five and seven litres of water a day. This was far more than is recommended, but I stuck to it religiously in the perhaps misplaced belief that it would help flush out the fat. I kept litre bottles of water at my desk, in the car, in bed – anywhere I knew I would be for more than a few minutes. Inevitably it led me to think that I might develop another phantom ailment – this time diabetes.

For the first few weeks I deliberately stayed away from the scales, anticipating the excitement of shedding the first few pounds. I felt better, cleaner somehow and more alive but also still lumpen. When I stepped onto the scales for the first time, filled with the excitement of having achieved something special, absolutely nothing had changed. The bathroom scales just crept up to the 16 stone 7lb mark, and did the same every time I got on them. More drastic measures needed to be taken. I returned to the diet list and crossed out the drink again, vowing to give it up for five days of the week. That way I could reward myself at the weekends. For the time being, I would continue to smoke but also tried to cut back on cigarettes, too. Not that I am sure it made any difference, but it felt like the right thing to do.

So much for the innards, but what of the body that I had to shed five stone from and needed to tone into coarse muscle and sharpened reflexes? In the modern era there are so many options for fat people to lose weight. There's a gym on every corner and swimming pools in every town. There are tennis courts and football pitches, bicycles, footpaths and now even government initiatives. When I put on my trainers for the first time, along with everyone else who was trying to make good their New Year's resolution, I joined the crowd at our local park as we did circuits panting, wheezing and sweating like old pigs ready for slaughter. I was grateful to be told by the racing professionals that I needed to protect my knees in order hold my balance in the saddle; it meant that running was out of the question. After my brief humiliation, I started cycling instead and quickly realized that it was the perfect way to combine exercising Billy.

Billy is a golden cocker spaniel. He was a gift from my mother-in-law and soon became a secret weapon in my fight against the flab. I had never wanted a dog, relenting only to please the children, but in time he became my best mate and a source of inspiration. He was an untrained, unkempt animal with awful, slothful manners. He was greedy, hardly house-trained, could be grumpy and misbehaved at every opportunity. We had much in common. As the weeks became months and I applied the discipline, slowly he came right.

Every morning I took Billy on the lead, towing him behind me while Lara, my daughter, rode her own bike. We soon got into the routine of cycling the three miles to Lara's school, although the first time we did this we were both nervous that Billy was going to end up under the wheels either of the bike or of a car, bus or lorry. But he got used to it and soon enough he was running alongside us, as we pedalled merrily past the morning commuters.

The weather throughout most of that winter was cold and crisp. I wore a beautiful brown tweed coat from Cordings of Piccadilly, more at home at a local point-to-point than Chelsea. Wrapped up in a puffa jacket and scarf, Lara would get dreadfully embarrassed because most parents either drove their children to school or sent nannies to escort them. After a few weeks, though, in a funny way she came round to enjoying the eccentricity of it all. Billy, on the other hand, loved it from day one. Cycling down long, tree-lined carriageways, over Chelsea Bridge, we'd stop to cross the main roads, waiting for articulated lorries to pass in a blast of diesel fumes. We took these opportunities to train Billy to sit and wait and for the lights to change before we get back on our bikes again. On the final leg of the journey we turned down Ebury Street and skirted Belgravia with people waving at us, cheering us as we arrived at the school gates. I would then chain Lara's bike to the railings outside the school until repeating the exercise later on in the day at 3.45, when I'd go to collect her.

From school I might go to the bank, Billy still in tow, or the butcher's, before returning home to stew some more lentils. Each time I cycled back on my own through the park I would pretend that it was a horse beneath me and not a bicycle and I would pedal furiously, overtaking Billy as he barked at me, feeling the wind in my face and knowing that every day I did this my thigh muscles would get stronger.

Working from home with Rose meant that we would meet for coffee after the school cycle ride and lunch together at 1 p.m. when we would routinely assess my diet and the exercise I was going to do. We quickly realized that the cycling alone was not enough, and so, twice a week, from the beginning of February, I took myself off to the Chelsea swimming baths just off the King's Road and put myself through twenty lengths of really hard physical swimming, resisting the urge to resort to doggy paddle rather than the really good heart-pumping stuff of front crawl and breaststroke.

One of the many benefits of the new regime is that I found mundane weekly chores much more enticing. Going off to the shops became a welcome distraction much more easily accomplished on a bicycle than in a car. As a result, as the new regime took hold I constantly found excuses to leave the house to go for a ride on my bike. I worked out that the long driveway running west to east in Battersea Park was roughly a mile long, so each time I left the house, no matter where I was going, I would always put in a lap of the track before returning home. I would step high on the pedals and start to push, pump and tug the handlebars as if they were reins. I would try to get the bike to go flat out and kept imagining, as on those journeys back from school, that below me was not tubular steel but a real, live, galloping beast of a horse, even though I had no idea when I would be getting anyway near one.

It was only a few weeks before I was sleeping more deeply, exhausted, but exhilarated, by the exercise. From about the second week of the diet I would wake every morning quite literally feeling things – toxins, perhaps – being expunged from my body. Although I already felt leaner – even if the scales did not say as much at that stage – almost the day I started the diet spots began to appear on my face as though twenty years of three-hour lunches and fine wine was seeping out of my body. It was as though my body was celebrating the change, enjoying the respite I was affording it and was preparing itself for the transformation that I was undergoing. Very soon after I started the regime, I ceased to have the urge to eat as I once had done, to drink or to smoke. It was as though the passion I had for all these pleasures had been transferred in one fell swoop to indulging none of them as I set about straightening myself out and getting fit.

By the end of the first month I had given up smoking altogether. Even at Christmas, I had been devouring thirty cigarettes a day with religious devotion even though I was not starting until after three in the afternoon. Like any good addict, I had quit on numerous occasions in the past and found it easy, but this time it would be different, I promised myself. This time I would quit for good, another positive side-effect of going in pursuit of this dream. The only problem, I knew, was that when I stopped smoking I would have to look for some other distraction. If I could channel that dedication into another kind of obsession, then I would easily be fit for a race day in September.

Chapter Two

I was six years old, completely enamoured and unable to move for the sight of it. I was walking with my mother through a mottled concrete yard near Mill Hill, an affluent suburb of north London. The treacly, ammonia smell of horse piss coming out of the stables that housed the horses filled the gullies and drains. Those aromas do nothing for some; others dislike them so intensely that it repels them immediately. I was overcome with delight. Even forty years later I can still smell it and I can see in front of me that little Exmoor pony, Conker, with his mealy muzzle and wonky trot.

Conker stood on a bed of yellow straw, behind a huge, creosoted stable door that he could barely see over, he'd rest his chin on the top of the door and look skyward. The straw was dusty but smelt fresh and I was timid in the company of this huge creature that stood peering down at me. In reality he was tiny but from the eyes of a six-year old boy he looked an equine giant. There was a water bucket that needed refilling and I opened the top latch and walked into the stable to reach it. I thought he would swing round and kick me but he didn't. Instead, he put his nose forward and nickered and nuzzled the top of my head. When I went to pick up his bucket he moved backwards so as not to frighten me. I darted out of the door, filled the bucket to the top with water and went back into his stable. He did nothing, just looked at me, then he came forward and put his nose in the bucket and gulped great mouthfuls of water. I backed away, still afraid that he might hurt me. His throat contracted and expanded as he swallowed the water, then he came towards me and slobbered water flecked with grain from his last meal all down my arm. I just stood there looking at him in wonder.

Conker wasn't the first pony I had come across but he was the nicest. He smelt like a bar of mouldy soap. I could rub my face in his mane, and my hands in his coat and they would come out covered in a sticky, waxy coating of scurf. It was one of the most delicious smells I had ever come across. He was small, just over twelve hands, and I would often ride him bareback in order to get the scurf to stick to my trousers so that I could smell them later and remind myself of him. He had a funny gait, almost lopsided, but he was very gentle with it.

Aged six, stuck in London and toiling with parentally imposed chores, I threw tantrums when it came to piano lessons and extra school tuition. The only place I wanted to be was in the stables with the horses. Such was my passion that once, when a great brute of a pony stood on my foot, rather than push him off I stood there wallowing in the pleasure of the excruciating pain. When I eventually pulled my foot from under his iron-clad hoof I saw that it had taken the skin off the top of four toes. They were bruised and bleeding but I was very proud of my injury, and for weeks afterwards I would look at the bruised and battered foot and think only of how much happiness the incident had given me.

'Why can't we live in the country, where the horses are?' I repeatedly asked my mother. Throughout my childhood I pestered my parents to move. Once, my mum drove me into the country and there, behind a post and rails fence, was the most perfect black Welsh cob I had ever seen. He was in a field with a ramshackle house next to it surrounded by acres of wide-open space. I turned to my mum and said: 'Are we coming to live here?' She told me that we were, 'But not just yet.' It was an unintentionally cruel thing to say, and it wouldn't have been practical, at least not for her. I, on the other hand, could think of nothing more perfect.

The most misguided hope I fostered was a return to Slades Farm in Somerset, to reclaim the family holding. My grandfather Percy had somewhat rashly let a part of it to the Bennett family, and with it the Bennetts acquired an agricultural tenancy – which could have lasted for generations. The three Hazzard sisters, of whom my mother was one, had been forced into the sale, in as much as they could not get vacant possession over the farm so it was worth considerably less than it might have been and consequently did not get a great price for it. I had been told the story of Percy many times, and even at the age of six I was already plotting and scheming as I had it in the back of my mind that one day we would return to reclaim what I saw as our inheritance.

At Slades Farm my mother and her two sisters had been brought up with horses, dogs, cows, pigs and chickens. When I did not grow out of the desire to bolt with terror every time I saw a dog – something that neither of my parents could understand – my mother, the psychologist, reasoned that putting me on a horse would overcome my fear of animals. And it did so almost instantly. What she did not reckon with, though, was that she ended up with something far worse than her small son bolting in a sweaty frenzy from a dog. With my new-found obsession with horses I lost interest in all things my parents valued, like schoolwork, the arts, reading and socially acceptable behaviour. But my fixation was not the romantic pony club schoolgirl type; it was a near-fatal mixture of love, hate and fear.

Long after I had stopped riding, in early 2009 a condition known as Equine Addiction Syndrome was coined by Professor David Nutt, the former drugs adviser to the Labour government of Gordon Brown. Equasy, as he named it, was responsible for at least ten deaths a year. According to his research, an addiction to riding horses was statistically far more dangerous than taking ecstasy or smoking cannabis. His rationale was that for every 350 exposures to the horse there was one serious adverse affect or injury, whereas for every 10,000 exposures to ecstasy there was only one adverse incident. His argument was simple: horse riding is more addictive and, indeed, more dangerous than taking Class A drugs. It was the same Professor Nutt who, also in 2009, raised the spectre that alcohol and tobacco were more dangerous than ecstasy. He was promptly sacked by a government that didn't like what it was hearing.

Although it took me years to articulate it fully, being put on that first pony, aged six, planted a seed that grew into an addiction the older I got and the worse the situation became at home. The musty, oaty smell of the beast and the heat that rose off it after exercise became entwined as a powerful symbol of all that I could trust and feel safe around while living a family life that was gradually getting worse with every passing year. There was a helplessness but also a fear of this animal that could, if it needed to, become ferocious. The anxiety many children show around horses is not cowardice; it is the same as that of the person who cannot swim and who has to jump into the sea so as to learn how to swim in case they ever get into serious difficulties. They may be nervous but they have to learn. That was how it was with me and ponies. But as I got to ride more often, so my confidence grew and I was relating more to horses than to home life, the family, school and people around me. But the problem I had was that we lived in London, not in the countryside, and it only became worse the older I got, and I was stuck with living out my dream watching horse racing on television.

Showjumping on the BBC was a favourite, and in 1970 I watched my first Grand National on television, sitting right up against the screen as though I might actually be able to climb into the paddock if I concentrated hard enough. Later, in 1971, watching Mill Reef winning the Epsom Derby was the first piece of real equine drama I witnessed, and the most exciting thing I had ever watched on television. The seventies were the heyday of British racing, and the country seemed to stop work weeks before the Derby, enthralled by the drama of the build-up. There were front-page headlines almost every day, and that year all the talk was of the little wonder horse called Mill Reef and his rich American owner, the banking heir Paul Mellon.

The television news reports called that year's race one of the finest Derbys ever run, and I watched it slumped in front of the television in a smoke-filled drawing room, staying with my mother's former neighbours at Gospel Ash Farm in Somerset. I was in horse heaven. Tiny Mill Reef, at barely fifteen hands, devoured the lush turf beneath his feet, flying over the ground before him, his rivals flailing helplessly in his slipstream. My heart pounded as I willed him to win. Away from my parents and surrounded by people who were just as fixated by the little horse as I was, I had never felt more at home. This was where I belonged.

After the race I went off with Victoria Gibbs to tack up her skewbald pony, Nugget. Even though it was mid-June, Nugget was covered in mud, having found a place out of sight in which to wallow and roll. The pair of us worked for hours scrubbing his coat, picking out his feet, sponging out his nostrils and eyes. I put his bridle on and he threw his head in the air as I tried to get the bit to connect with his mouth, but I was only nine and quite short so every time he wanted to avoid the bridle he just lifted his head up in the air, knowing that I wouldn't be able to reach, even on tiptoes. He blew out his stomach as we tried to tighten the girth straps. Victoria and I trotted off down the flint-strewn track and I worried about Nugget's feet; he had no shoes on and was uncomfortable, often darting onto the grass verge where it was softer underfoot. When we got back my hands, pullover and jeans reeked of Nugget.

Riding Nugget during the holidays, I was happy beyond anything I had ever experienced. At the end of the summer we would return to London and that irresistible waxy smell would fade from my clothes as we drove east towards London along the A303. I was not enamoured by the prospect of the drudgery of London life and the world that I inhabited, as a suburban child, with no horses in a stable outside the back door. I knew, like a person who feels he is in another body, that I was growing up in a wrong place. If I had been born a generation earlier I would have grown up with the animals on the farm, horses, hunting and racing. As soon as we got home I shut my bedroom door and lay in bed longing for the day that we could return to the farm and I could get back in the saddle.

*   *   *

Chiswick Comprehensive School was in the same league as Holland Park Comprehensive. A former grammar school, it was staffed half with old-school grammar school teachers and half with right-on lefties. I started there in 1972, aged eleven, with children of other parents who also should have known better, among them the sons and daughters of politicians, academics, doctors, lawyers, film stars and businessmen. I hated every minute of it. The problem was that all the children were guinea pigs and the parents were indulging themselves in a socialist experiment that for a lot of us turned out to be a complete disaster. My mother told me years later that the comprehensive system was a 'brave new hope' that was embraced by all right-thinking parents.

The teaching was truly appalling but the politics of the time dictated that the system and the school would work perfectly. No one, least of all the parents, was looking at what was going on and I ran riot at every opportunity. I was constantly being caught smoking, bunking off to go and ride and very often just not bothering to turn up at all. Following my dad's diagnosis, my behaviour spiralled out of control. I couldn't and wouldn't concentrate in the classroom. Homework was abandoned amid great tantrums, and it took very little for me to start playing up as I moved listlessly from one term to the next, only just avoiding being expelled.

Locked in my bedroom as punishment for yet another misdemeanour, I wrote stories about horses and executed very bad paintings of them, too. It seemed that it was only when I was in the company of horses that I calmed down, and I took every chance I could to return to the stables in Harefield where my pony, Bracken, was kept at livery. The only one who put his finger on the personal issues I had was our physical education teacher, Mr Reynolds, a tall, athletic man who loved his job. He once said to my class that there was only one boy, in his opinion, who would ever be as passionate about what he did in later life as he was. He knew I was flailing around at school, but he could see that I had a passion I couldn't yet fully articulate and he had faith that I would eventually come good. It was a strange moment: I knew that out of all those children sitting in front of him in that class I gave him the most grief, and yet he chose to praise me above all of them. There were others who were not so kind: the French teacher, Mr Bumford, who one day for no apparent reason came and stood on my fingers as they were splayed on the floor behind me. Even my classmates were shocked.

Everything changed when, aged twelve, I met Emma. One year above me, Emma Burge was small and blonde and, like me, horse-mad. We started bunking off school together, went riding, smoked Silk Cut Blues. I tried to sell an Oxo cube dyed with green ink as a lump of hashish to some of our friends. And almost every minute that we were together was spent talking about ponies.

My first entrepreneurial foray was not a great success and I had to return all the money we'd earned when the deception was uncovered, but Emma gave life at school a new dimension. Her parents had a house in the New Forest where Emma kept her pony, a fiery upstart called Fred, and a donkey called Jasper. Turned onto his back and held down by local farmhands, Jasper used to have his ever-growing feet clipped so that he could walk comfortably. At weekends we would go down and visit and Emma would drive Jasper and I would ride along beside her on Fred as we ambled through the New Forest. We had much in common since her parents understood nothing about horses either, and I was saved from myself, at least temporarily.

Emma was the first girl I fell in love with. One of the wonderful things about her was that she always washed her hair with Brut shampoo; sportsmen like Henry Cooper, Kevin Keegan and Barry Sheene were famous for advertising Brut aftershave during that period. It was really cheap stuff but Emma managed to make her hair smell incredible whenever she washed her hair with it, and I would hold her in a boyish embrace and nuzzle her hair, inhaling the scent, just as I had done with Conker. When we eventually drifted apart I would sometimes buy a bottle of Brut just to remind myself what she smelt like. More than thirty years later, Emma is still crazy about horses, but now she has stables of her own and she drives the horses competitively.

Emma and I went our separate ways when she was sent to Dartington Hall School, a wayward and very costly institution in Devon, while I stayed at Chiswick for another agonising year. Although we stayed in touch, Devon was a long way away for a twelve-year-old. She made new friends, but occasionally she would turn up in London and we'd talk about horses, smoke a bit of dope and reminisce about the ghastliness of Chiswick Comp., and then she was gone again. She got married at nineteen to a wheelwright and they went to live in Wales. The marriage only lasted a short time and produced a baby. One day, fed up with the life of a wheelwright, Emma jumped on board Fred the pony and rode him about two hundred miles from Wales to the New Forest, where her parents still lived, with the baby strapped up in front of her. She could have gone by car but loved the pony, and didn't want to be separated from him. That's what horses can do to you.

While I was tearing the school apart, able only to concentrate on horses, my parents' main concern was my father's health. It was not the first time illness had stalked the family. My brother Rupert, born in 1963, very nearly died before he'd even got started. Water on the brain made his head swell to gargantuan proportions, which engendered a very strong protective love in my mother and meant that more often than not I was left to my own devices. Meanwhile, the pain got worse for my father, and he stubbornly kept to his walking stick even though it was obvious to everyone around him that he should be in a wheelchair. His muscles started to seize up and once he was mistaken for a drunk as he stumbled along the pavement willing his legs to work. There were pills and potions, too, and, early on, he drank vast quantities of sunflower oil. Research had suggested it might help with the symptoms and I willed it to cure him.

As I struggled through my teenage years, so my dad's decline became more rapid, until he was spending a lot of time in hospital undergoing one test after another. Going to the John Radcliffe Hospital in Oxford to collect him, following yet another day-long examination, he was sitting, a stick in each hand, still just able to shuffle around a bit when I arrived. He was surrounded by wheelchairs, and people so crippled by disease and so obviously in pain and distress that it was difficult to lift my eyes off the floor. This was what was going to happen to him and I couldn't bear to look. I asked him how his tests had gone 'Well,' he said, at the top of his voice, then pausing for effect, 'they said if I was a racehorse they'd have to shoot me!' He roared with laughter. The other patients were not so amused.

I left school as soon as I could, just after my sixteenth birthday and before they threw me out. In the hot summer of 1977 I shaved every last hair from my head and turned up at school the following day, surrounded by crowds of admiring friends, and was duly frogmarched from the premises. I was at last free but prospects were pretty bleak. An O level in English Language was the sum total of my formal education.

My parents had dreamt of me going to university, but from where they were sitting prison looked a more likely option, conflict abounded and we were never far from a row or argument about my lack of progress. At least I had an entire summer with horses to look forward to. During those long and painful months, my mother, who had just about given up on me, happened upon a course in Horse Business Management at an agricultural college in Witney, Oxfordshire. It was a rare moment of understanding between a sixteen-year-old and his forty-nine-year-old mother.

The drive to Witney on that hot summer morning was memorable, largely because my mother and I were filled with hope and optimism for the first time for as long as either of us could remember. All was not lost, and she had finally got the message that it was with horses that I was happiest. The course she had found would let me spend every day with horses learning how they worked. I would be taught about veterinary medicine, breeding, nutrition and the racing industry.

I studied under the tutelage of John Onions, a man who single-handedly changed the course of my life. Onions looked like a hobbit and had huge enthusiasm for the horse business. He knew its foibles and machinations and he also knew just how complex an industry it was if you scratched under the surface. I was taught alongside a journalist from the *Sporting Life*, various sons of farmers, an insurance broker and lots of pony-mad girls who were always phoning Mummy from the college call boxes to check if Moonshine or Dobbin had been fed. I felt I had arrived in a world that I'd been searching for for years.

I lodged with Professor David Fieldhouse and his wife, Sheila, at Lower Farm in Leafield, a few miles outside Witney. A tidy, utilitarian smallholding with horses and cows, it was a perfect rustic idyll. But there was an intellectual element prevalent, too. David was Professor of Colonial and Naval History at Nuffield College and brought a rather stern rigour to the breakfast table every morning. A prolific scribbler and studious intellectual, he encouraged me to write. As I sat puffing on cigarettes, putting words down on a clapped-out Olivetti typewriter in my bedroom, the scales began to fall from my eyes. David would correct the English, punctuate the prose and push me along, all the while smoking his pipe. The Fieldhouses' politics were about as different from my own parents' as it was possible to be and lodging there gave me my first exposure to another way of life.

It was while staying with them that I was introduced to the showjumping correspondent for the *Daily Mail*, who had been a stable lad himself and knew a great deal about horses. In time I managed to supplement my meagre income at the stables by penning articles for *Pony Magazine* and *Dog International*. The first fee I received was £100, enough to cover my board and lodgings for a month.

The atmosphere at Lower Farm was both bohemian and agricultural. Everyone in the family rode and, each morning, I would help them mucking out the stables and feeding the horses before attending college, and then again in the evening before taking one of the horses out for a ride. I loved the routine, and, for the first time in my life, didn't have to be bellowed at to get out of bed in the morning. Instead, before breakfast, whatever the weather, I would wait for the rest of the family to get up before we walked over to the stables and groomed, picked out the horses' feet and tacked them up.

In the winter Katy, their youngest daughter, and I would go hunting and in the summer to pony shows, and the problems at home seemed like a distant memory. Meanwhile, my father was becoming increasingly curmudgeonly, with even his politics veering alarmingly to the right as he got angrier and angrier as the illness took hold. I struggled to understand what he was going through, but having gone deaf at twenty-one and then developing multiple sclerosis in his forties, it was no wonder that he was raging at the injustice of it all.

Following college, a job riding and breaking in young horses beckoned – but I got into trouble again almost immediately, primarily because I did not get on with my employer. The family I worked for in Buckingham didn't like the rough-hewn manner that I affected. There was a 'them and us' divide, and if something was wrong with a horse you went to the back door of the big house, once used by the servants, to tell them. In the morning horses were tacked up for the master, his wife and daughter. Manes and tails were brushed out, hooves picked out and oiled and then the animals were paraded in front of them. For my part I did not like the way they treated the people who worked for them. They viewed their staff as an underclass and wanted me to become a member of it. There was an argument, words were spoken and I returned to my parents' home jobless. After the magic of the previous year, it was an unexpected setback as my mother sighed, wondering what she was going to do with me. Exasperated, she gave me an ultimatum. Be in a job within a week, or they would no longer house me.

That was more than thirty years ago. Aged nineteen, I weighed close to 10 stone and could ride a horse well. I could canter, gallop and jump large fences, and was one step away from making the move into a life surrounded by horses. Jobs with horses were then, and still are, badly paid. Conditions are treacherous and I had very little to fall back on if I didn't make it. In a rush of blood to the head I abandoned the ambitions for a life with horses and instead took my Olivetti to London. I have been there ever since.

Chapter Three

Six weeks into the new regime, Ralph, who had been best man at Rose's and my wedding, came to visit with some much needed encouragement. His weight, too, is prone to ballooning since he has an appetite for food, wine and cigars to match my own. However, without telling me, in the past two months he had given up carbohydrates, cut down on wine and managed to lose two stone. He is about to reach forty and I guess he, too, is feeling that mortality is catching up on him.

We had a takeaway curry from Exotika, but no bread or popadoms. I had a green chicken masala curry, Ralph a jalfrezi and we consumed a handful of onion bhajis between us, all washed down with plenty of wine, which I justified by saying that I had not drunk all week. At the end of dinner I took a few puffs on Ralph's cigar but didn't like it. During dinner he was positively effusive in his praise of the progress I had made, although I pointed out that I hadn't gone anywhere near a horse yet. It was encouraging to hear, though, that I was changing shape. Of course, like other friends, Ralph thought the project a little dotty. Years before, I used to ride with Ralph at his mother's estate in Italy, to where I had exported from England a band of very well-bred Connemara ponies in order to establish a stud. Ralph was useless on a horse, but utterly fearless even though he had great goofy teeth and very bad sight. One day we were hacking in the hot sun through olive groves when a piece of gravel shot up from the rear hoof of the pony I was riding straight into his eye; it got under his contact lens and he screamed and shrieked like a wounded animal. His eye streaming, he begged me to stop, so we did. He abandoned his pony, Cuckoo, right there and then.

The day after our dinner, I was racked with guilt at having strayed from my monastic diet, and determined to redouble my efforts. I cycled twice round the park and made a real effort to puff myself out. I stood up on the pedals, Billy running furiously beside me, trying to keep up as I stretched my legs and felt muscles that I forgot I even had working away under the flab. I did an extra lap of the park as Billy tried to drag me home, and could feel the muscles in my legs aching when I got down off the bike. Even three weeks before I would not have been able to do that. Back home, I gobbled a small portion of linseed and barley for breakfast and a plate of lentils for lunch, cooked in chicken stock until they were firm and crunchy.

As well as upping the mileage around the park, swimming at Chelsea baths was now becoming a daily event. It is an old municipal-style pool with a spectators' balcony running down one side. The pool is set out in lanes so only those serious about exercising go there, and there are no diving boards or water slides, so there are no children to get in the way. I plunge into the medium lane, the water is lukewarm and I set about my target of twenty lengths.

For the first five lengths I go flat out, stretching my arms and kicking my feet, taking deep breaths to expand my lungs and undo the damage that the smoking has done. Pushing against the water as hard as I can, exhaustion sets in and I slow the pace for the next five lengths, then I try full exertion for two lengths before slowing down again. I know if I were doing the exercise on dry land I'd be soaked in sweat, and with a lean lunch in my belly it is not long before I can feel the fat burning off me. The water keeps my temperature down and I can feel my heart pumping through the ripples. Back on the bike for the cycle home, my legs ache and I struggle to ride in a straight line. The discipline is marvellous, and six weeks in a proper routine has developed, all of which makes me wonder why I hadn't started doing this twenty years earlier.

While Rose has helped me put the diet together she still brings home mouth-watering food to feed the children. To start with I was able to sit at the table with them as they ate, strong-willed enough not to be tempted to pick at their leftovers, or to find an excuse for just one small mouthful of succulent beef. By the end of February I had lost around seven pounds (or fourteen packets of butter, as I preferred to view it) and could feel that my clothes had loosened around my girth. But I knew myself too well, and could feel the temptation threatening to get the better of me. So I found ways to distract myself while the children were having dinner. I would find an excuse to be on the phone, take the dog for a walk – anything that would keep me out of the way of Mr Robinson's sausages. In the past, as plates of delicious food were put down in front of the children I might occasionally take a mouthful of sausage from their plates, or a slice of tender chicken. Not now, though. When they ask me to come and sit with them I might finish their greens, which I know are good for me and they can't stand.

I weigh myself every day, and eventually the needle starts to creep back anticlockwise from 15 stone 10, where it had been stubbornly fixed in the first few weeks. As I stand, I practise pushing my knees together as I have been taught to do in preparation for riding. The trousers aren't pinching as much as they did even a week ago and I already feel much better, with all the exercise and the fresh air that is now filling my lungs. The time has come to sit on a horse and start riding for the first time in twenty years.

I last got on a horse when I was twenty-eight, on a trip to Ireland. Next to me on the plane was my most recent (and very tricky) girlfriend and ahead of us was a new adventure and with it the hope that this would be the beginning of something special. I had been sent, in the middle of a bitter winter, by the *Evening Standard* to write a piece about property in Ireland, a country that was in the depths of recession and twenty years into the Troubles that began in 1969. I had little interest in the piece but knew that it was an opportunity to indulge my passion for horses, and my fixation with the girl sitting beside me.

At Dublin airport we hired a car and drove to Mullingar, Co. Westmeath. I had a week to write the piece, and I decided it could wait. I had been offered a day's foxhunting by a former Master of the Westmeath Foxhounds, and I could not possibly refuse. Hunting in Ireland was something I had never done before, but had always wanted to. My girlfriend, a lissom blonde, was at heart a girl from the shires, horsy to the tips of her upper-class toes. How she would admire me, I imagined, as I took those vast Irish walls at full gallop in pursuit of a fox. How brave. How handsome … I could not wait to show off.

Hunting in Ireland was something that all horse types aspired to. Its stone walls, open ditches and the fast galloping pace was a very different affair to the more sedate hunting fields of England, and offered everything that I loved about being on a horse. The day before the hunt, with my tutor, a grand horseman called Frankie Kiernan, we rode out to get acquainted with the countryside and to shake off the staleness of the working week.

My horse, a beast of an iron-grey gelding named Zachariah, was, at just four years old, much younger than the horses I had been used to, but his behaviour belied his youthfulness. A Thoroughbred crossed with an Irish draught (a carthorse to you and me) standing around sixteen hands high, he was perfectly bred for the job. His predominant gene being Irish draught meant that he was calm and unflustered but at the same time he moved forward nicely and seemed unperturbed by the jumping experience, traits unusual in a horse so young. He had also just been sold to my friend's brother-in-law in England and he was due to be shipped over to Wiltshire within a matter of days. While he was inexperienced, a few words from Frankie reassured me. 'If you try and hold that fella up like you're doing you'll get into terrible trouble.' But I had an audience to impress and I thought I knew everything there was to know about horses, so I was trying to get the horse to bounce in front of the open ditches we were practising over, and then leap like a stag over them. Frankie pulled me up immediately. 'The only way to ride open ditches is at a fast gallop,' he said. 'Just lean over him and let him go'. I tried it Frankie's way and it worked a treat. Zachariah galloped and galloped and we flew round fields, over low stone walls and wide drainage ditches. London, the *Standard*, the job I was meant to be here doing seemed a million miles away. It was everything I hoped an Irish hunting adventure would be. My girlfriend was deeply impressed too, cooing over me for the rest of the day, so proud to be on my arm.

That night we drank and ate like kings. At that time there was none of the virgin olive oil or lattes of modern Ireland. We filled our bellies with home-made soda bread, Irish whiskey and rubbery Gubbeen cheese. Fish was in abundance and the meat was good, too. I had a few Irish whiskeys then steak, potatoes and, of course, bottles of wine. Before I went to bed I laid out my hunting clothes – breeches, a tweed jacket, hat and long black leather boots, which I waxed and polished until they shone. In the morning I washed, drank a cup of thick brown Barry's tea and swallowed a mouthful of soft soda bread spread with salty butter. While I waited for the rest of the house to get ready, I paced up and down, hoping that the day would live up to expectations.

I rode down to the meet, and among the thirty of us gathered there was a hunting priest on a piebald cob. Schoolchildren, who should have been in class, were mounted on hairy ponies. Farmers on Thoroughbreds arrived with their wives on Irish draught horses, and rubbed shoulders with the sons and daughters of wealthy parents on flashy animals, all wanting to get on with the day. This was a ragbag of individuals, all gathered with one aim in mind – to chase a fox. I wasn't nervous, just rather delighted that I was combining a passion for the horse and work at the same time. This was the beating heart of rural Ireland at its most glorious.

The Ireland of thirty years ago was a country where, if a wall fell, it was up to riders to close the gap using barbed wire, and where nature was allowed to overflow unchecked. Anyone out riding had to pick their way through acres of unkempt land, keeping a careful eye on where they were going. I trotted off with Zachariah as though we were old friends. He stopped and started and galloped at my instruction, like a gentleman waiting for me to tell him what to do next. We went through gateways and cantered up hills. He broke into a sweat but never appeared anxious. He was going to look after me was Zachariah.

As the morning went on and I became more confident I tried hurdling larger and larger obstacles. Jumping off a bank down into a riverbed, Zachariah stumbled but collected himself quickly and went on cantering through the water and scrambling up the other side. He was as taken by the occasion as I was, but although he was just as excited as me he wasn't pulling, and would always wait for me to guide him before starting his gallop.

I had noticed that some of the other riders were jumping barbed wire fences, which I had avoided to begin with, having never jumped them before, but as the day progressed so my courage grew. A barbed wire fence is probably the most difficult thing a horse will be asked to jump. It is vertically upright, difficult for the equine eye to discern and, if you become entangled in it, it cuts you like cheese wire. As I sat watching the others jump over the wire, I thought they were mad, but earlier someone had hung hessian grain sacks and plastic fertilizer ones over the barbs so that the hunters wouldn't cut themselves if they dropped a leg low when jumping, and they didn't seem to be having any problems.

By lunchtime we had tracked a fox, the hounds were in full cry and were in full flight across the open fields. As we galloped to the top of a wide-open hill, we were confronted by a large wall. Horses were stopping and refusing to jump. Some approached, then, losing their nerve, ran out to the side. The wall was around five feet high, the same height as others we had cleared easily all day. Emboldened by how well the morning had gone so far, and egged on by some of the field, I said I'd put Zachariah over and the others could follow. The only shame was that the girl I'd come out to Ireland with was nowhere to be seen; she was going to miss my finest equine moment.

A mother and her daughter were queuing up behind me. They knew Zachariah and assured me he'd 'pop over' the wall with no problem. I agreed wholeheartedly. We turned a circle, broke into a canter and went steadily towards the wall. Any rider will tell you that you only ever realize how big a wall is when you're bearing down on it, the full scale of it only becoming apparent in the split second after you have left the ground. Just as we were about to take off, I realized that it was much bigger than I had anticipated, but I need not have worried as Zachariah leapt beautifully. In that moment I became calm again, thinking that, while I was not in complete control, at least Zachariah was. I loosened the reins slightly and I gave myself over to him.

On top of the wall, unseen, lay several strands of barbed wire. Underneath me and out of my sight, Zachariah's front hoofs clipped the coping stones on top of the wall and he scooped up the clawed wire with his forelegs. The pain must have been unimaginable, and he was still rising, gathering momentum as the spikes started to take hold of his forelegs, tightening with every centimetre further that he travelled. I looked to the right to witness fencing posts pinging out of the ground before they broke and splintered around me. Then it was happening on my left as well. As we landed, a dollop of metallic-tasting blood hit me in the mouth. I was in big trouble. Zachariah and I were the stone in a lethal barbed wire catapult. The mother behind me shouted at her daughter not to watch. 'Look away,' she cried, as I was battling to steady Zachariah, as the wire tightened and the ground in front of me turned red. He started bucking, trying to free himself of the wire that was cutting deeper and deeper into his flesh, as it took hold around his neck

Zachariah bobbed one way and twisted another and then the wire wrapped itself round my left knee. As he bucked ferociously beneath me, I was trying to get off to calm him down and all I could think of was that this poor young horse was going to die under me. But not before he had torn off with my leg wrapped in the wire, losing a limb as half a ton of horse hared off, dragging me behind him by the leg. I looked around, shouting out for someone to help us, but there was no one there, the mother and daughter having disappeared from sight on the other side of the wall.

Like a bronco in a rodeo, Zachariah took one last corkscrew of a turn. He bucked so high that the wire ran down his neck and ripped a two-inch hole in the toe of my boot, slicing straight through the leather, but miraculously missing my toes. There was blood everywhere, pumping out of Zachariah's neck, covering the ground and mixing with the sweat on my face. This was not how it was supposed to end. I was twenty-eight and about to die, and taking a borrowed horse with me. I'd done nothing with my life. I didn't want it to end like this.

In a final leap, Zachariah flung me from the saddle and galloped off down the hill, blood pouring from his neck with yards and yards of barbed wire and fencing posts chasing after him. I was shaking, near-hysterical. A man galloped off in hot pursuit of the still bleeding Zachariah. The mother and daughter gathered round to comfort me, and ask if I was OK.

I just shook, unable to move. All the joy of the morning had evaporated in an instant, rich pleasure turned suddenly to horror.

Zachariah was eventually caught. I ran down the hill after him, stripping off my thick tweed jacket as I went. He was standing, shaking, sweating and frightened. I tied the jacket round his neck like a tourniquet, pulling it tight to stem the bleeding. We were only half a mile from home and someone called a vet from a nearby farmhouse and asked him to get to the house to tend an injured horse. We couldn't decide whether to wait for a car and trailer or just run back. Zachariah was in shock and I decided to lead him, trotting back to the stables, thinking all the time he was going to die on me, right there in that lush country lane. The blood was still seeping from his neck but I took solace in the wise words a vet once uttered to me: 'If a horse severs an artery he's usually dead within forty-five seconds.'

Zachariah was still with me. I pounded down the lanes, egging him on to keep up, all the time thinking he would collapse. The vet was waiting, with a drip to pump an iron solution into Zachariah and slowly he began the delicate process of patching him up. There was nothing more I could do. I went into the house, poured a large whiskey, smoked a cigarette and I never got on another horse again. Zachariah survived.

My girlfriend left me not long afterwards, and for the next twenty years I couldn't bring myself to get back in the saddle. And this was the problem. I had not ridden a horse since then, and, to be frank, was still terrified that the memories of Ireland would come rushing back at me the moment I got back on a horse. To do this properly and not get spooked I was going to need a plodder, a horse that could get my confidence back. But where would I find a horse that would look after me, and who would be mad enough to lend me one?

Chapter Four

A year before we married, Rose and I were looking for a house to rent in Dorset. I had rented a small cottage on the Rushmore estate on Cranborne Chase for several years but it was little more than a 1950s semi-detached prefab. In the winter it was wet and cold, and even in the summer the landscape was devoid of all joy. With no garden to speak of, it was little more than a bachelor pad in the countryside.

Teddy Bourke and his family own the village of Chettle, which borders the Rushmore estate in Cranborne. It was in stunned amazement that Rose and I traipsed up through the woods on the outskirts of the village one Saturday afternoon to look at Keeper's Lodge. In a clearing stood a colonial-style bungalow, a former gamekeeper's cottage built from brick and flint more than 150 years ago, nestling on the boundary of an ancient woodland. To say it was both beautiful and tranquil would be to misrepresent it. Keeper's Lodge is unique. On our first viewing, as we opened the back door a herd of sheep ran out of the front. The grass around the house was knee-high, birdsong, like some distant melody, butterflies fluttered in the sunlight.

The house was gas-lit and was little more than a scruffy oasis in the midst of an overgrown wilderness. But it was perfect. There was – and still is – no rubbish collection, no postal delivery, no proper road and very few services. In the village there was a stable full of horses, and in August 1993 we took on the lease. We have been there ever since.

The children have had the benefit of growing up both in London and in a wild place with woods and birds and cows and farm animals and a small shoot that I run. Except for the supply of electricity, which we now have (don't let anyone try to convince you that gas lighting is romantic: it isn't) and an unkempt garden, not much has changed in the seventeen years we have been here. Friends in the village have married, given birth and died. People have come and gone but all around Chettle is an untouched idyll. Together we have shot the deer that roam in the woods, the pheasants that sit in the hedgerows and the partridge that squat in the barley fields.

Kevin and Rose Hicks have been in Chettle as long as we have and live for horses and little else. When we visited, the stables held a mix of big, hefty hunters, ex-racehorses and a small Shetland pony called Mandy. Aged five, Lara used to go down to the Hicks's yard in the village to groom her. Just as I had done as a child, she would lovingly scrub all the mud off her, sponge out her eyes and ears and pick out her feet. Then we'd tack her up with her saddle and bridle and off we'd go for a stroll round the village.

It was to Chettle that I retreated for the winter half-term in February to get the first taste of what it would be like to get back on a horse. Apart from the occasional slip, when I gave in to the temptation of a groaning dinner table, I had managed to stick resolutely to the diet despite the shaking of a few heads of those who still could not believe what I had got myself into. I had lost just over half a stone, and was lighter now than I had been for ten years. The circuits around the park that were getting faster had given me enough confidence to think that I was making the necessary progress to pull this off. All I had to do now was get on a horse and be able to stay on it through a walk, a trot, then later a canter and a gallop.

For every rider, being on a horse is all about the gallop. It is instant gratification. It is also daring, exciting, exhilarating and dangerous, very like the way most riders like to live their lives. I don't think an accountant has ever galloped; neither has a man who digs the road for a living. But the journalist who has just landed the big story is at it full pelt. Footballers gallop, the ones playing on a Sunday at the local rec and the ones playing in a cup final at Wembley. They gallop. It's daring and emotional, and it is also draining. I knew that if I could learn how to gallop on a horse again then I would be some way towards getting myself out of this midlife crisis slump. Some men in the same position leave their families and disappear with young girls; others buy yachts. I have no inclination to do either.

The first port of call on arriving at Chettle, already dreaming of putting on my racing silks, was to Kevin and Rose. They were aware of my little adventure, but I was unsure how to broach the subject. You don't just lend a horse to a 15-stone man and wave him off down the lane.

Ever since I've known Kevin and Rose I've assumed that all Rose's horses are either deaf or impervious to her screaming and hollering: 'Get up, you fucking bastard, or I'll have you' is typical of the sort of riposte she often makes to an equine miscreant. Not only that, Rose also likes to ensure that anyone within half a mile can hear her telling her horses off. They do, because you can't help but hear her when she hollers. For a woman, her expletives are quite extraordinary. I start telling Rose about the idea of my race and I can see she is quite impressed. I have yet to find a trainer, but she offers me her own retired racehorse, Edward, to exercise. 'He'll carry you, even at fifteen stone,' she says.

On the face of it this is a great idea as Edward is in the village and I can ride every time I'm here. I say 'on the face of it' because it is only later that Rose tells me, 'Edward bucks a bit, oh, and he can be a bit strong. But don't worry, you'll be all right.' 'A bit strong' means that I won't be able to stop him until he has galloped all the way to our nearest town, Blandford Forum. 'Bucks a bit' means that he upends himself onto his forelegs, puts his nose between his legs and tries like hell to get rid of his rider.

I decided not to take up Rose's kind offer, at least for the moment. When I got home I enquired at the local riding stable about the possibilities of riding one of their horses. I was cut short before I had a chance to deliver my full pitch about fulfilling a childhood dream, and was told in no uncertain terms that I was not going anywhere near their stables. This was a riding school, not a circus, I was told. I put the phone down, wondering where to turn to next.

I opted to take up Rose's offer after all. So, most mornings we rode out. Edward was fine; he didn't buck, he moved forward fluently. We had a great time in the early mornings, slow, long canters, pheasants shooting out of the hedgerows. Walks and trots and talking all the time about riding and racing and Rose side-eyeing me as if to say, 'You really are mad, you are.'

On the first Sunday of our stay, after walking Billy we were invited to Cranborne for lunch by some old friends, the Campbells, who lived in a house almost as charmingly dishevelled as our own. The drink flowed and the food, piled high, was brought to the table. I made a vague gesture of waving away a second helping before giving in, thinking that as soon as I got on a horse I'd be able to burn off the excess calories twice as quickly. We feasted on rare roast lamb, crisp, succulent and bloody, potatoes, spoonfuls of cheese and great hunks of bread. Dessert was a crumble with cream; there were flagons of wine. By the end of the afternoon I could feel myself bulging out of my shirt once again, like a character from a Thomas Hardy novel.

Bloated and content, I waited for the appropriate moment before telling the assembled company about my endeavour.

'I need to ride a horse, every day', I said.

It was a sort of 'my kingdom for a horse' moment when George told me that I could exercise her horse, Daz, which was stabled at her brother's house in Cranborne, a ten-minute drive from Chettle. Perfect.

George Campbell has no fear of anything, least of all riding horses, and she loves to get her friends involved in her equine exploits. She once pleaded with me to allow her to take Lara out hunting. Envious of her fearlessness I almost agreed, thinking it would be a great thing for a pony-mad girl to do. It would be the ideal opportunity for her to experience the rush of adrenalin and fear that I hoped she would come to love.

George's husband, Mouse, however, had other ideas. He kicked me sharply under the table and mouthed silently, 'Do you not know we are in the presence of a mad lady here? Under no circumstances should you put her in charge of your only daughter on the hunting field. Do *not* do it.' There are quite a lot of people in Dorset who agree with Mouse. And, as I was to find out later, when George is on a horse she knows only two paces – walk and flat-out gallop. She has suffered innumerable broken bones and bumps to the head but when

I ask her if she ever feels nervous she says, with a huge, haunting grin sweeping across her face: 'If it's meant to be it's meant to be.' And, of course, she has a point.

By early March, two months after I started the diet, I had already lost three-quarters of a stone and was feeling much better for it. It was a moment of truth as Jack and I drove to Cranborne to meet Daz. She was a sweetie. Horses are measured in hands, from the ground to the bottom of the neck, and a hand is equal to four inches. Standing at over eighteen hands, Daz was a Thoroughbred-cross shire horse, and towered over both of us like a benevolent giant. She was such a big animal that I had to use a stepladder to get onto her and I knew that if I came off I wouldn't be able to get back on again.

I looked around for my jockey skullcap, something you have to wear by law when exercising racehorses. All I had on was a flat cap that I liked to think made me look like the late, great Sir Noel Murless, one of the few jockeys in the history of the turf to have been knighted, and latterly a Newmarket trainer extraordinaire as well as being patron of and mentor to Lester Piggott. But that is where the comparison ended. Sitting on top of Daz, I realized that it was a hell of a long way to the ground. If I came off her and landed on my nut it would not be remotely amusing, but George told me that it was an absolute rule that if I rode Daz I had to wear a flat cap, not a skullcap. When I mentioned that if I fell off and landed head first on the tarmacked lanes of Cranborne, my children would be fatherless, she laughed. George didn't even wear a helmet when she was pregnant with her daughter Martha. I now understand more fully why her husband didn't want her to take Lara hunting.

My dad used to drive me mad about the type of headgear I rode in. He would read every technical report in every scientific journal that warned of the perils of the common-place fibreglass hunting hat with the fixed peak. With great amusement he would read out the reports citing fractures that might splinter and end up embedded in the forehead of the rider. In the mid-1970s his advice had been that I should ride in a helmet favoured by Securicor delivery drivers, with a thick mattress to protect the back of the neck and a visor to cover the face. This did not go down well with me. Part of the attraction of the horse is the inherent danger, but the fact that equestrian headgear has been drastically modified since I was a child is not lost on me. My dad was right, I was wrong. Still, what I remember loving about those early days with horses was being at a gallop and feeling the wind in my hair, with a complete disregard for any health and safety considerations.

It is only when I was firmly on top of her, with no easy way down, that George told me Daz was blind in one eye. No one seemed to know much about her, bar the one irrefutable fact that she did seem to be a very kind old lady. But, like a lot of kind old ladies, she had her nasty streak and hers was that she did not like going through gates. This made me nervous. Every time we approached a gate she would back off very quickly and her front legs rose just a little off the ground, which caused me to lean forward and grab anything I could to stay balanced on top of her. I sensed that she'd had a previous punch-up with someone at a gate, and had probably been walloped around the head with a stick once upon a time. She needed to be cajoled and stroked and caressed, not beaten. When I was younger I would have been inclined to give her a bash with a stick, too, but, at the age of forty-seven, I don't carry a stick and she did seem to respond to kindness, not brute force. Any physical confrontation with her would be laughable since she was probably ten times stronger than me, so I sat quietly in the saddle and waited for her to make up her mind.

Apart from going through gateways she was very willing, and as we cantered slowly along the soft track high on the downs overlooking Cranborne, I was back where I was as a child. The smell of her was both rough and agricultural, yet she was kept in five-star conditions. She was stabled with other horses in a small block with a deep bed of fresh straw put down for her every night. A net full of sweet hay hung from the stable wall for her to pick at, which supplemented her diet of concentrate foods, oats, barley, maize and bran, which she was fed twice a day. There were always two full buckets of water for her to quench her thirst. She was turned out into a paddock every day. In the summer there was sweet, lush grass for her to graze and in the winter she was given an overcoat to keep her warm. She was tended and cared for by a resident groom, Trina.

As we made our way through the countryside her ears pricked up as she took in her surroundings. It was easy to forget that it was only through training and trust that she didn't do one of many unthinkable things such as depositing me on the floor, and on that first morning out I had to make a good job of not thinking about her rearing up and throwing me off backwards.

In order to stay put I started by riding with very long stirrups, which went against every piece of advice that trainers and jockeys will give you. The shorter the stirrups the better the balance, but the deeper I sat in the saddle the more secure I felt. It was only much later that I gained the confidence to shorten the stirrups and keep my balance with my knees. For now it was enough just to be back on a horse.

Back in the stables after my first canter I could see just how far I needed to travel in the next six months to pull this whole thing off. Daz was not bullet-proof, that much was now clear, and I was certainly not bomb-proof. At 15 stone, even getting off her was something of a challenge, and I held tightly onto Daz just in case something went wrong.

For the next month I came down to Cranborne every weekend and got to know Daz. As March gave way to April, the harsh winter was replaced by a miserable, overcast dampness. When I returned to Dorset from London to ride out on Daz, the drizzle was like wet cobwebs. On first arriving at the cottage I would light the wood burner and then feed it up with coal and lay a fire for my return. Out of the freezer, usually stuffed to the gunwales with partridge, pheasant and other game, I retrieved some frozen chicken stock, took an onion and a packet of lentils from the larder and left them on the counter for when I got back.

Ordinarily, when I got to the stables Daz was resting on her hind legs, watching me with her one good eye. I took her rug off, gave her a quick rub down and put on the saddle and bridle before walking out into the beautiful yard where the gardeners and craftsmen would be tending the lawns and laying new paths among the huge avenue of beech trees. The turrets and the gardens of this extraordinary manor have seen countless prime ministers as guests over hundreds of years, and it has been the scene of many plots and much political planning. Mrs Thatcher, John Major, Chris Patten, Princess Margaret and many more have all stayed there, but the secrets of what was said remain behind its battlements.

The Cranborne estate has also been in the Cecil family for an equally long time. George understands well this world that she has been born into. Every morning starts with a visit to the stables, and it is easy to see why the horses here appear to be so happy. Her brother rides too, but he does it not because of the lure of the horse but for the danger and the rush of adrenalin that comes on race day. He likes to compete in point-to-points, the brain-damagingly danger-ous pursuit whose origins lie in racing horses exactly as the name suggests – from one point to another. Although, like me, he tends to run to fat, he adores this pursuit and antici-pates the start of the point-to point season with great pleasure.

When I talk to him about the plan for my own race he offers me a grim warning. He tells me that when he was useless, the other jockeys used to laugh at him, but as he got better they became nastier. In one race he took part in they tried to run him into the side of jumps and unseat him. They swore at him a lot and generally made his life as an amateur jockey as unpleasant as possible. 'Enjoy it, but be warned!' he tells me before I head back to the stables. I am not sure how competitive I am likely to be, but I heed his warning in any case.

Along with our passion for horses, we share a rather eccentric way of losing weight. When I saw him earlier in the year he told me that he had the perfect diet: 'Plenty of whisky and lots of steak.' He claimed to have lost several stone this way. His sister confirmed the diet but added that it gave him terribly bad breath, and then roared with laughter as if to say that I, too, was afflicted with halitosis on my diet of grains but she was just too polite to tell me.

Each morning I clambered on board Daz, patting her and talking to her as we went. As we headed off through Cranborne I would call 'Good morning' and 'Lovely day' to passers-by, and then we would take a left fork and follow the track onto the downs. We'd have a trot and then a slow canter, when suddenly a pheasant jumping up from the hedgerow would cause Daz to flinch before tightening up again. She bunched her haunches beneath me but I'd pat her and talk to her quietly and soon enough we would be on our way again as her fear subsided. I kept an eye on her ears, though, the best way to tell her mood. As with any horse, when they are laid flat back on her head she is furious; pricked firmly upright and she is happy and enquiring.

We cantered up the hill, past abandoned pigsties and hedgerows that were pushing into bud and then bloom. As we turned the corner to the left her ears were firmly pricked, and I was settling into the rhythm of a rider. And then, in a flash, she started again, this time more abruptly, and I was cast all the way back to Ireland. Daz had spotted a tractor harrowing the soil on the far side of a barren field, its driver entirely disinclined to slow down. This was what I had been dreading: a great jangling monster coming towards her. I am not sure who was more frightened. Daz pricked up her ears even more – they were now like stalks as she fixed her eyes on the huge chain harrow. Then she splayed her legs and froze. I prayed and started making preparations for how to deal with falling off and I braced myself for the worst. Sure enough, Daz swung sharply to the left and took a pull on the reins. My worst fear was about to be realized: Daz was going to take off at a flat-out gallop down back towards Cranborne. After taking a great heave and a pull on the bridle she veered off, back down the hill towards the village. I was shit scared, convinced that I was about to meet my end. I started loosening my foothold in the stirrups, preparing to jump overboard in the hope that she would stop when I did so, since if I did jump I'd be bound to break a limb.

Then, God intervened and Daz started to calm down and she let me pull her up. I turned her back towards the tractor, whispering words of encouragement to her as I tried to make sense of her fear. I rubbed her shoulder and, replete with a new-found confidence, gave her a gentle slap down the neck with my stick, squeezing my legs with all my might and then prodding her in the ribs with my heels. She veered left towards the fence on the other side of the track, but not so near that the wire would cut into my calf. Our confidence now restored, I felt that I had her under control again and that I could convince her to do things my way. I could have panicked and shouted and frightened her but I didn't; I sat tight, in control and all the time pushing her forward, onward. This was a good sign. It's different if you are with someone else when this kind of thing happens, but if you are in the middle of nowhere on a huge horse and something goes wrong when there is no one there to help, then it is the loneliest place in the world. I am, after all, responsible for her, too.

Then I patted her and gathered up and shortened my reins and we were off into a slow canter, the tractor and harrow far behind us. We were alone now, meandering through open gateways, along tracks, passing by barns and farmyards and then back through that dreaded gate. I reached down for her sweaty neck and told her we were nearly home: 'Just this last gate, Daz.' She knew that through that gate there was a bed of deep, fresh straw and a net full of sweet hay and a bowl of grub. For a horse it was the human equivalent of walking through the doors of the Savoy hotel. So she went quietly through the gateway and on we pottered down the High Street and onto the gravel path. Then it is just down the garden path with an arc of pruned and trained trees inches above my head. She was tired and I was aching but finally we got there, and in one piece. I slid down off her back and banged down onto the gravel. Kissed her and put her to bed. I was very, very happy.

I drove back home to Chettle and reported my act of supreme bravery to Rose, Lara and the assembled company in stopping the runaway steed and narrowly averting an accident. My daughter likes to mock me and, true to form, she immediately roared with laughter, lowering her head towards the floor as she mimicked a plodding old carthorse. She then told everybody present that it was her impression of Daz and that her old dad was living in a dream world of his own making. Everyone laughed. I walked into the kitchen and got on with cooking my lentils, ignoring the mockery.

It was coming on. I was back on the horse.

Chapter Five

Four months into my adventure and I am back in London standing naked in front of the bathroom mirror. I run my fingers across my face, and I can feel immediately that it is not so saggy. The spots that had broken out in the first weeks of the new regime have disappeared, the heavy jowls I had got used to and had felt quite attached to have started to recede as my jawline has begun to emerge again after more than a decade in hiding. The stomach is not as pronounced and the thighs feel tauter and bulkier. Before I started the diet I had never been terribly interested in my body, and this is the first time I am paying any attention, maybe even too much, to it as I go through this routine every morning looking for signs of improvement. While more people are commenting on the new me, what they can't see is the work that is going on beneath the surface. Even in three months I have changed. I feel stronger, healthier – lighter – than … well, it has been so long that I can't remember any more.

Tentatively I get on the scales and shut my eyes before looking down. They tell a good story. I have lost just over a stone. Looked at another way, my body has shed the equivalent of twenty-eight packets of butter or seven bags of granulated sugar. I think it is an achievement, since it is the first time in my life that I have lost weight, not found it and clung to it through all the excesses. But there is still something not right. It's the drink, I think.

During the first two months I had still been drinking. Nowhere near as much as before, and certainly not a bottle or two a night, but when the weekends came I really went for it. A diet has to be taken in stages, I reason, and anyway Rose shared the bottles with me. But I vow to cut back even more. The potatoes, pasta and white bread have long been a thing of the past, though. Rose has allowed me to have a small amount of brown bread because, she says, as the flour has the husk still on it should be fine. I pretend to understand why this should be the case and put it down to the husk being roughage, so the body can process it more expediently and flush it from the system.

So far so good. However, I have still not got around the issue that the portions Rose continues to serve are gigantic, even though I feel as if I am eating less. On the few days when I pass on the lentils and fish for something altogether more sumptuous, I can see that each helping could serve at least two, maybe three, people at a time. Needless to say, it doesn't matter how healthy the food is: large portions and greed are not good bedfellows for someone on a diet. Memories of an old photograph I once saw of Lester Piggott dressed only in a bath towel in a sauna with a plate of lettuce, a glass of water and a cigar in hand come back to haunt me. I bring this up with Rose at dinner, and the children stare at me in disbelief. After all, not that long ago I would put one plateful away before coming back for seconds and thirds. When Rose ordinarily serves dinner she piles huge amounts onto my plate and around half that onto hers. Weary of asking for equal portions, I deftly swap plates. This avoids rows and arguments about portion control which I want but she doesn't.

The cycling regime is strengthening my thighs and calves, and I have increased the mileage to five or six laps of the park, much to the confusion of Billy. When we get back home now he is more exhausted than I am, and immediately retreats to his basket for the rest of the morning. I take this to be a good sign. However, even after having gone for a few canters with Daz I know that I am going to have to crank it up even more in order to be properly fit. To lose a stone is something to be proud of, but I have to shed at least another three to have any chance of competing in a race, and, as anyone will tell you, the first stone is always the easiest to lose.

At dinner one Saturday night, the second bottle of red already opened, I announce that I am going to give up drink altogether – but after Easter. The children scoff. 'You don't believe me?' They both shake their heads. 'I have lost a stone already, you know.' They look at each other in disbelief and carry on eating. This is getting too much. I get up and pull out the notebook in which I have been documenting my diet and exercise regime and each log of my decreasing girth. 'Look. It's true.' There is nothing like children to strengthen one's resolve, and I realize that they are probably right and that I need to double my efforts. The aim is to be 13 stone by mid-May then 12 stone by August and to maintain that weight until my race, date as yet to be confirmed. As the children get ready for bed, I return to my diet book and make the necessary readjustments.

Monday to Friday	Water, tea, linseed and barley for breakfast. Lentils, pulses or beans for lunch with meat, fish or eggs. Meat, salad, cheese for dinner. Tea and water to drink only.
Monday to Friday	Cycle five times around park except Wednesday when cycle six times around. Swim vigorously forty lengths and sauna twice weekly. Bathroom floor exercises twice weekly.
Saturday and Sunday	Water, tea, bacon, eggs, sausages, black pudding. Salad and fruit for lunch. Meat or fish for dinner with lentils, pulses or grains. One glass of wine only.
Saturday and Sunday	Ride Daz as often as possible when in Dorset. Cycle on Saturday. No exercise Sunday.

Below this I make a note to myself that I need to have a trainer in place by May.

But (and it is a huge but) things can go wrong. The discipline and concentration needed to maintain control over outside influences and distractions is enormous. Daily I am tempted to eat something I shouldn't, not to bother about cycling, to give swimming a miss. But generally, miraculously, I don't. The closest I come to returning to the bad old days is three hours into a *Private Eye* lunch at the Coach & Horses, Soho. Thankfully the food is not up to much, and the wine stays mostly at the other end of the table. The table just sniggers when I proclaim that I have lost a stone. 'Where?!' they laugh. They laugh even more loudly when I tell them of my intentions. 'Is this a substitute for a mistress?' someone bellows from the end of the table. I restrain myself from pointing out that more than one of them has taken that more conventional route down the path of a midlife crisis. We sit there for a bit and I tease Ian Hislop about his shiny new suit. When I ask him if he has a television appointment later in the day, he smirks. Francis Wheen often teases him about needing a chauffeur, such is his elevated position. We repair to an upstairs room for a cigarette where the mocking continues, and I am asked to show again how much weight I have lost and the size of my stomach. Wheen mentions that the columnist Peter Hitchens had lost stones by eating only kippers and cabbage. 'It might be possible, I suppose,' he mutters before lighting yet another cigarette and pouring yet another glass of wine for me.

The following Saturday, a wet, windy and uncomfortable day, we hold a '*Daily Telegraph* Christmas' at Chettle. The purpose of this is to re-create our family Christmas for the newspaper's magazine for one of the issues out in November. Rose is writing the piece and the children are being photographed. Jason Lowe, a master of his craft, comes to take the pictures. George, the keeper of my beloved Daz, is coming, too, with baby Martha and husband Mouse, and they are all keen to find out what progress I have made. Having taken rather badly the need to show the children the diet I am on, for the sake of the photo shoot the diet is put on hold. 'It's Christmas, Dad, you're supposed to enjoy yourself,' Lara says, patting my stomach. Rose agrees, thinking that it would be monstrously unfair to let me watch them indulge in roast goose with the trimmings, while I have to stick to lentils cooked in chicken stock. I can't say that I am overjoyed: the menu looks delicious, but deep down it does reinforce the promise to double my efforts once the plates have been cleared.

The day starts well enough. Jason erects a huge arc light outside the cottage, pointing directly through the window. Cynthia, the stylist, has driven all the way from London in a large white Mercedes with no reverse gear and packed to the roof with props. There is endless sitting around waiting for the room to be dressed and then the children get restless and start to run off just as we are about to sit down to eat. Meanwhile, the dogs tear around trying to pull the goose from the table and it is several hours before calm is restored. By this time those of us adults who are waiting around have already made our way through three bottles of wine and, while I feel guilty for three seconds, I am soon reaching for the corkscrew and can see no irony in the fact that all I can talk about is how much I want to compete in the race.

In the space of one afternoon, between five of us we manage to demolish one goose, one ham, fourteen bottles of fine wine, a bottle of port, fruit and cheese. We then play Monopoly as if it really were Christmas, pull the crackers and then open some more wine, the only mishap being that we all get too pissed. Plastered, I trip over and land on a stone trough in the garden, cracking a rib. It is too painful to laugh and impossible to cough without a searing pain ripping through my left-hand side. A cracked rib is a classic jockey's injury, and the irony is not lost on the assembled party. Apart from strapping you up, there is very little a doctor can do about a fractured rib apart from telling you a. that it is broken and b. that it will take a long time to mend so I decide against hospital. Rose thinks the fracture is hilarious, telling me, 'It serves you right for getting so pissed'. Riding Daz will have to be put on hold for a couple of weeks.

Three weeks later I can still only get out of bed by rolling onto one side, and the children have great fun trying to make me laugh so that they can watch me double up in pain. The telephone goes and I manage to get out of bed on the fifth ring. It is Trina from Cranborne asking why I haven't been down to see Daz recently. I tell her about my trip, explaining that I am out of action for a short time. I promise to come and visit as soon as I can.

It's only when I get to Cranborne that Trina tells me I'm not the only one who has been laid up injured. Daz has not been ridden since I last came to the stables because of a sore leg. She can detect my anxiety and can see that I am picturing her giving me a two-hoofed boot in the air that would send me flying before depositing me on the other side of the stables. I clutch my chest, but, while it is still sore, I am able to ride, and when we finally get out of the stables and walk tentatively down the track, as we have done so many times before, I tighten the reins instinctively, even though I know this is not going to do either of us any good. But if she is as spooked as I am, she doesn't show it, and gradually I calm down.

We have a long, steady canter up a flinty hill on the downs. Halfway up I ask her for a bit more acceleration. Riding her is rather like driving an old automatic car. She starts well, glides smoothly as she accelerates, but she gains speed a little lumpily and there is no great surge as she goes through the gears. Perhaps it is the 14½ stone that is preventing her from careering off into the distance. She is indeed a very sensible old lady, and I feel I can really trust her with my life. I rub my hands on her sweaty neck and pat her warmly as she slows down to a walk. As we round the corner at the bottom of the hill, Lara, my daughter, is sitting under a verdant hedge waiting for us both to come home.

Four weeks after tripping over, the rib has healed sufficiently for me to be able to ride Daz out twice a week. I have
managed to stay away from the wine and am actually really
enjoying the diet, which has forced both Rose and me to be
more creative in the kitchen with the ingredients that I am
limited to. The possibility of becoming a jockey is starting to
become a reality. More than twenty years after my ill-fated
trip to Ireland the tweed jacket that I had used to stem the
flow of blood from Zachariah's neck still hangs on the back
of a door at our cottage in Dorset. It has seldom been worn
and still bears the stains of battle. The boots with the toe
ripped off sat for years rotting in a barn. I have still not
thrown them away, but I haven't worn them since.

And yet, even though for all that time I was unwilling to
put my foot in a stirrup, I kept being pulled back to horses.
No matter that I refused to ride again, at every opportunity I
talked about horses, talked to them, sized them up as I tried
to get inside their heads to work out why one horse might be
quicker, sleeker, fitter and psychologically better balanced
than others. Perhaps it is precisely because I could not bring
myself to get back in the saddle that my obsession took hold
to such an extent that virtually my entire professional career
became dominated by horses. Now, though, that is no longer
enough. The time has come to return to them and begin my
search for a real racehorse and a race – and for that I need
someone who really knows horses and how to get the best out
of them. It is an art of which I have been a student for years,
and a skill that comes naturally to very few people.

* * *

During the spring and summer of 1989 I made a documentary film for Channel 4 about a rag-and-bone man, or totter, called Markey Bernard and his horses, which he stabled under the Westway flyover out of London at Shepherd's Bush. Markey was the best horseman I had ever come across, and he would have been the first port of call in getting race-fit. To travel out to the underpass with the traffic heaving out of London above us was to experience a peculiar confluence of countryside and city that seemed to exemplify everything that my life had become. Every time I went to see him break in horses and ride and drive them in a cart around the streets of London it reminded me that I was the wrong person living the wrong life.

Markey had been born in a stable under the flyover, and came from a long line of totters. When I met him he was in his fifties; he was stout and physically incredibly strong, with a huge appetite. On the days I spent with him we used to go totting together, stop off at a café in Ladbroke Grove and leave the horse and cart outside while we went in to consume the most enormous breakfast. While we ate, the horse would stand outside, unhitched. I once asked Markey why he didn't tie him up and he said, 'Oh, don't worry about him, he won't go anywhere.' That to me was magic. Here was a horse which would obey a man, almost through telepathy.

During the weeks I spent with Markey I realized that what I needed more than anything else was a horse of my own. Ruby was a Welsh cob with a rich black coat. She was beautiful. Not long after I bought her she won a rosette in a local pony show in Dorset and I sent her to Markey to be broken.

It was around this time that I started courting Rose. One rainy Sunday morning after our first date I took Rose to see Markey and Ruby. I'm still not sure if she could believe that, for a date, I was suggesting not a nice lunch at a restaurant or a stroll in the park, or going to see a film or meandering round an art gallery. Instead, on a cold, wet November morning, I was offering to take her to see a horse under a flyover in Shepherd's Bush.

Markey had taken delivery of Ruby just three weeks earlier. She was an unbroken three-year-old, and ordinarily it takes around six months to change a horse from wild miscreant to obedient servant. We arrived and Markey said, 'It's OK, you can drive her.' So we tacked her up, harnessed her to a trolley, oiled her feet and set off along Scrubs Lane. Her coat was gleaming, her body had filled out and the truant behaviour that all horses arrive with had gone. Guiding her from the cart, we trotted along safe in the knowledge that Markey was next to us, should something go wrong. At first, Ruby wasn't easy and she shied a bit, still getting used to being instructed, but slowly she got the hang of it.

And then, as the rain lashed down, and we reached the junction at Latimer Road, she spotted a manhole cover next to a bus stop where people were sheltering from the rain. A bus drew up beside us, applied its air brakes and Ruby leapt in the air, stepped then skidded on the manhole and ended up in the bus shelter, scattering the queue down Latimer Road. We were in trouble. Markey came to the rescue, hauled her off the pavement with a mixture of guile and brute force, and we were on our way again. Back to the yard, hot, soaked and slightly shaken, Rose, not a horse fancier, hadn't flinched. Markey took me to one side and said, 'She's a good girl, you should marry her. Better than the rest you've brought down here.'

Rose had grown up with horses, and when we met I assumed that I would have another chance to show off my equestrian prowess once I had summoned the courage to get back on a horse. But Rose could not have cared less about them. As a child she had listened to endless dinner-table debates about martingales and bits and fetlocks and pasterns. At weekends, protesting furiously, she was dragged off to gymkhanas, pony club events, hunt races and point-to-points. While others messed around in stables, she stayed indoors indulging her interest in cooking.

More than anything, though, horses terrified her. She had seen, first hand, what an obsession with horses could do to people and families as her father had frittered away most of his cash and time buying hunters, stables, horse trailers and lavish amounts of food and hay for them. He had even contrived to run off with a female groom in his employ, having previously left Rose's mother for Annie Lou, who was also horse-mad. For Rose, then, horses meant trouble and she was unable to grant redemption for that folly even all those years later.

Markey would have enjoyed the journey that I was embarking on. Illiterate, he lived in a very different, more brutal world from the one that had sprung up around him. He had forgotten more about horses than I would ever know, and long after the film had been finished I would drive over to Shepherd's Bush to watch him drive his horses. In the evenings we would retreat to the pub where he was treated like a king. Those who did not know him knew of his reputation and I would take a kind of childish pride in sitting with him as others pointed in our direction, whispering to each other that this was the great Markey Bernard, king of the totters. Markey died of cancer in 1995. I visited him once in St Mary's, Paddington, but then I couldn't bear to see another sick and dying man and he passed away without fanfare. After that visit I never saw him again, but those who went to the funeral told me that it was a grand affair; a glass hearse drawn by two fine black Welsh cobs took his coffin to its final resting place. There would never be another like Markey, and so it was to a more traditional racing master that I would have to turn for help.

Chapter Six

No matter how good a rider you are, if you want to be a jockey you first have to find a licensed trainer. You cannot just go out and buy a horse and race it yourself. Find the trainer and he'll find you a racehorse. Once you've found the trainer he has to give all the undertakings about your competence as a jockey, sign the forms and enter the race for you. There is no better place to start looking than Newmarket, a small market town in Suffolk and the capital of English horse racing.

The first weekend in May sees the running of the first Classic races for three-year-old horses, the 2,000 Guineas and the 1,000 Guineas. Held at Newmarket, these are the first really big spectacles of the flat-racing season. It is here that the superstars of the turf emerge. For several years now at the start of the new season we have stayed with Diana Cooper, one of the most well-connected people in English horse racing. Diana oversees the two-year olds in Sheikh Mohammed's vast Godolphin Racing empire. We arrive on the Friday evening at her Victorian villa on the outskirts of Newmarket. The house belongs to the Sheikh, one of the richest and most powerful men in the world, who happens to be Diana's friend, too.

Diana knows just about everyone in the horse racing world, and it is safe to say that if there is a trainer she doesn't know then he or she probably isn't worth knowing. She has been a part of this world all her life. She was born into it and lives and breathes the sport, and she is a fantastic hostess as well. Her fridge is always fully stocked with food and her cellar contains some good Burgundies and some serious Bordeauxs which I manage to avoid.

For our arrival she had prepared an enormous spread of oily smoked salmon with brown bread and lashings of butter. Roast chicken and simple roast potatoes and a lemon juice- and olive oil-dressed salad were then brought to the table, all of which I picked from with great restraint, much to Diana's surprise. Some of the fine wines were served and these were followed by oozing, soft and stinking cheeses. They sat on a plate at room temperature, huddled up in curds and rind, and we ate them with biscuits, bread and lashings of salted butter. The knife sliced effortlessly through one piece of delicious, creamy cheese after another until we were bloated and could eat no more. Afterwards, Diana, a seasoned campaigner, joined me in a cigarette or two and when I finally made it to bed it was in a state of exhausted delirium.

Saturday morning was bright and spring was now on full parade. Out of the kitchen window I could see blossom on the trees, and bacon was sizzling away in a brand new super-non-stick frying pan on the Aga. There were warm bacon sandwiches and mugs of tea for everyone, and while I held out for a moment the smell was simply too good to resist and I sunk my teeth into thick slices of home-made white bread (brought by us from London) and bacon held together with giant slabs of salty butter. There was no denying that, compared to my usual breakfast of rolled oats, crushed barley and linseed, this was a feast.

I drove to get the papers from the tiny village shop in Moulton and we sat crouched over the kitchen table studying the racing form, drinking coffee and smoking cigarettes, the first packet in months that I had opened the night before. While the house got ready, we contemplated the next two days of racing. At 12.30 we donned our fancy clothes. I put on a very conservative blue light woollen suit, a simple silk tie with an understated pattern and loafers, offset by red socks, while the ladies changed into tight dresses or shimmering skirts.

Newmarket is the home of flat racing in Britain, and it was where my journey to find a trainer would begin in earnest. Punters, owners, trainers, jockeys and spectators all descend upon the course, flood the grandstand, drink champagne, scoff burgers, loiter in boxes overlooking the track. The track is about more than just the horses. What attracts such large numbers of people who have never gone near a horse before is the camaraderie, the friendship, the speed, the death-defying exploits and above all the passion. There is, of course, also the betting. Every year people come to Newmarket with the dream of their horse running that bit faster than the others. It might mean enough money to pay for a fancy meal on the way home, a new car, or, if the odds are really good, and the punter brave enough, it could mean paying off the mortgage.

When we arrive, Newmarket is bustling with chavs from Essex in their stretch limousines hired for the day, trainers in their trilbies and their wives in chiffon dresses and jewels, as they wander between the paddock, the bookies and the hamburger stands. While there are class distinctions, and the extraordinarily rich rub shoulders with those far less well off, they are all here for one reason: the love of the horse.

The sun shines and the course is lit by a bright glow that covers the huge expanse of the famous Rowley Mile. This year, like every other year, we have an invitation to the Tattersalls box, which overlooks the winning post. The boxes either side of us are occupied by Sheikh Mohammed and Weatherbys, the racing secretariat. John Magnier, the arch maestro of the bloodstock world, and his cronies lurk upstairs. Pretty much the sum total of British racing is around us, certainly the majority of the most powerful people in the horse racing world. This is horse racing's equivalent of standing in the directors' box at Manchester United listening to the musings of Sir Alex Ferguson and the first team squad. While we wait for the races to start, all the talk is of buying and selling horses, insider tips, gossip and questions about which horse is going to gallop home with the greatest prize in English horse racing, the Derby. Tattersalls are the largest bloodstock auctioneers in Europe and have sold a number of Derby winners, and every-one keeps an ear to the ground as soon as they enter the grandstand in the hope of picking up a vital tip.

The favourite for the feature race of the day, the 2,000 Guineas was New Approach, owned by Sheikh Mohammed's wife Princess Haya of Jordan. The Sheikh had purchased 50% of the colt eight months previously. It then promptly won the Dewhurst Stakes at Newmarket and the Sheikh fancying his chances at a bigger prize promptly bought the remaining 50% that he didn't already own. In total the horse had cost him £15m and this is the edgy difficult to train equine that all the punters have come to see.

The 2,000 Guineas is run over a straight mile and is treated by many as a preliminary race for the English Derby. That being the case the Sheikh's £15 million looked ill spent. New Approach came second, being pipped by the Aidan O'Brien trained Henry The Navigator. From the balcony I peer out at the vista that disappears into the distance where, soon enough, jockeys will be jostling each other for the best line along the finishing straight. I can feel the blood rising to my head at the thought that in six months' time I will be one of those jockeys. Perhaps not here, but on a racecourse somewhere, head down, horse beneath me, making the final charge for the finishing post. I reach into my pocket and pull out another cigarette.

While the punters stand around admiring the horses and the jockeys in the winners enclosure, the real kingmakers of the paddock are the trainers. Like film directors, they bring order to the chaos. The horses, some of them at least, will become the stars but only for a relatively short time. By contrast, the trainers are really the ones who matter, and it is their names that people remember. Henry Cecil, Aidan O'Brien, Sir Michael Stoute and Sir Mark Prescott, to name just a few from among the legions of trainers, have established a certain longevity. In their eyes the jockeys are simply the men who steer the beasts on their behalf, and they see very little difference between a good jockey and a great one. What matters is how the horse is trained and who has trained it. These special few dictate the rise and fall of almost every jockey.

One of the legends of Newmarket is Sir Mark Prescott, with whom I made a film about the last Waterloo Cup, the blue riband of hare coursing, now banned. Dating back to 1836, with its origins in Altcar, outside Liverpool, the race used to take place in the open countryside and pitted two greyhounds against a live hare. The hare was rarely caught but when it was it was dispatched pretty swiftly. Prescott has trained horses for almost every race in the world and yet he says that he would sooner have won the Waterloo Cup than the English Derby. I wanted him to be my trainer.

Although he is one of the finest exponents of getting a horse to run faster and longer and with more passion than most trainers, Prescott is essentially an outsider at Newmarket. He is a strict disciplinarian but also a libertarian, who runs his yard and trains his horses in an almost Victorian way, and he doesn't socialize with other Newmarket trainers, preferring to spend his spare time going to the theatre or watching bullfighting and boxing. Just to be in his presence inspires a sense of occasion, and when I went to see him I found myself hanging onto his every word. I knocked on his door on the pretext of wanting to find out more about the world of trainers; however, what I really hoped was that, once I had explained my idea, he would let me ride one of his horses. The last time I visited him was when Lara was seven and he had given her a guided tour of Heath House. This is something that Sir Mark rarely does, but when I told him how horse-mad she was he agreed. We saw the stables, stroked the horses and visited the huge barn where the younger horses were being ridden by lads and lasses in order to prepare them for their first races. Outside we had watched as he coaxed three horses through the freezing cold equine pool, where they were being pushed and cajoled and learning to strengthen their muscles. Then Lara was introduced to St Simon, regarded by many, Sir Mark among them, as the greatest racehorse of all time. To be more precise, she was shown St Simon's skin, which hangs in a gigantic frame just outside the barn where the horses are trained. Undefeated on the track, he went on to be the leading sire for nine seasons during the late nineteenth/early twentieth centuries. His skeleton belongs to the Natural History Museum in London.

For Sir Mark Prescott the act of training a horse is a repetitive exercise that has intrigued him for more than forty years. While the science of horse racing has done little to improve their overall speed in two hundred years, the challenge for Prescott is to know how much faster than the competition his horse can run to be sure of winning. It takes months of planning, plotting and fine-tuning. And even after that, and a lifetime of study, his winner to runner ratio is only around 30 per cent, which is still about 200 per cent above the national average.

The morning I went to visit him, the yard was as immaculate as ever. The grass was manicured, the woodwork was glossy green and had just been repainted, as it has been every year since he arrived in 1970. The horses looked out over their doors and there in front of them stood the great man himself. All bonhomie, he strode towards me along the yard, his neatly combed hair swept back off his face. A giant Monte Cristo protruded from his lips, and a large plume of blue smoke swirled around him in the gentle breeze. He inhaled deeply before extending a huge welcoming hand.

In one crucial respect the art of horse racing has not evolved one jot. Unlike in almost every other sporting endeavour, man has never been able to get the racehorse to run significantly faster than he did for his forebears. Hundreds of years ago the horse ran just as fast as it does today. Compare that with human marathon runners, who improve their time on an almost annual basis, and the record for short-distance sprint races like the one hundred and two hundred metres, which is regularly broken. This is a strange

state of affairs and one that has puzzled generations of trainers, vets and spectators. Prescott has a view on this: 'It is the
conceit and vanity of the athlete that enables him to run ever
faster and break more records. Equally, it is the will of the
dog to stick its teeth into the little white arse of the rabbit it
sees bobbing up and down in front of it that makes him run
faster. But the horse has absolutely no incentive to run faster.
We train horses because there is an industry built up over
three hundred years that demands it. If I said to any of my
horses "Would you like to go racing today?" they'd say, "No,
thank you very much, Sir Mark, I'd much prefer to stay in my
stable and eat. But do please be my guest, take that little
jockey you were hoping to put on my back, head for the races
and have a jolly nice time."' While I take his point, I am not
sure that Prescott is entirely correct here because, barring a
few exceptions of a horse's bad behaviour, when a horse gets
to the track it seems to me to be very keen indeed to get on
with the job.

For all the money that is spent on horses, there is very little
science applied to the process of training horses, just gut feeling. Being trained drives many horses mad. It is the job of the
trainer not to overdo it. The ticks and curious habits that
some horses adopt are a result of the extreme pressure they
are put under by the trainer and the environment they live in.
Horses show it in lots of peculiar ways. Some wind suck –
quite literally sucking great gulps of air into their stomachs.
If a horse does this it reduces its value at auction dramatically.
Others bite into the stable door, or walk manically around
and around the stable, knocking anything, including men,
out of the way, and others weave from side to side. A horse
bought at public auction with any such vices can be returned
by the buyer straight to the owner.

In the early 1980s, along with my cousin the psychologist Jon Beer I undertook some research into stable vices, which was funded by the National Trainers Federation and published in the racing industry magazine, *Pacemaker*. We discovered that the most expensive vice was rug chewing, whereby a wintertime-rugged horse tries to remove its overcoat, often worth hundreds of pounds, with its teeth. Although this might cost the trainer a great deal of money, it actually has no effect on a horse's performance at all – nor on its value. But take a horse that wind sucks or cribs or weaves and its price is immediately halved, for no apparent reason. They are no more difficult to train, they are no more or less successful: they are just worth 50 per cent less than they would be without the vice.

It's the same with physical abnormalities. If a horse has a parrot mouth, meaning it has an overshot top jaw, this has no effect on its performance, little effect on how it eats and no bearing at all on its mental or physical wellbeing. Nonetheless, these horses are nearly all worthless. To an outsider this might seem like a very strange way to do business, but trading in the horse world is carried out in pretty much the same way as it has been for hundreds of years, and when I bring it up with Sir Mark he just shrugs.

With the half-idea that, because we get on so well, he might – just might – say, 'I've got a horse for you', after he has shown me around the yard I broach the subject of my race, and the real reason I have come to see him. 'I want to become a jockey and try to ride in a race. I wondered if that is not something that might entertain you and whether I could come and work for you for free.' I add, for good measure, that I think I can sort out my own board and lodging and that I'd be no burden. I promise that I'll work hard, turn up on time and do as I am told. A huge wave of optimism engulfs me as I make my pitch and wait for his reply.

He roars his head off and says, 'I will not entertain show business jockeys in my yard, sorry. I'd love to help but it's not for me. It'll be a great thing to do and I wish you well; it'll be great for horse racing.' To be fair, looking at me waddling towards him, all beer gut and fat rolling over the trouser line, I can't really blame him. Prescott is small and lean. He walks with a slight stoop, a legacy of when he was a jockey himself and broke his back and had to spend nine months flat on it in an orthopaedic hospital. He had been told not to expect to walk again, let alone ride. What was I thinking? Of course he wasn't going to let me anywhere near one of his horses. I would have to find someone closer to home to train me, and I had just the person in mind.

*   *   *

Every time we go to the Guineas meeting at Newmarket, for some unfathomable reason we win money and usually lots of it. That year was no different. We picked up tips for the following day and then in the evening, after the first day's racing, we returned to Diana's house for the most spectacular fiftieth birthday party for her brother Alan, who is racing manager for the super-wealthy Niarchos family. The food was delicious, the wine of the highest quality and we danced all night, rubbing shoulders with racing's elite. There was a purposefulness about my dancing, something that I am not usually keen on, and in the steamy confines of the marquee I felt that I was being put through a proper workout.

For much of the evening I sat next to a charming French trainer called Pascal Bary who had a runner called Natagora in the following day's 1,000 Guineas. I asked Pascal whether his horse was going to win and he said, 'You can never tell with horses, but I would say that she was worth a flutter.' I thought that was as near a sound piece of investment advice that you could get.

Later in the evening, I told Pascal that I was going to become a jockey. He looked at me for a very long time in complete silence. Then he took hold of my arm, and leant in with a face of complete seriousness. Did I know what it entailed – the sheer physical effort, the starving, the early mornings? Did I know how likely it was that I would get seriously injured? All this I had yet to contemplate, but I knew that sooner or later I was going to have to take the plunge and give myself over fully to the life of a jockey. It would not be an easy thing for a metropolitan man like myself to achieve, he offered. Smiling, he looked me up and down, gesturing with his hands in a classically French manner: 'Anyway, you are zee wrong shape.'

The next morning started early with a cup of tea in bed. A hearty breakfast followed and off to the races we went again to plunder the previous day's winnings onto Natagora. We were not disappointed as she romped home. We gathered up our winnings – nearly £600 – and headed off back to London singing made-up songs about the horse as we sped down the motorway. To celebrate our winnings, and to toast the horse, we decided to make one last stop before we got home. Driving onto the Commercial Road through the East End, my mind full of the week's training already planned out, we just couldn't resist it and, prompted by Lara, we decided it was time for one last visit to one of our favourite restaurants. We stopped at the Lahore Kebab House and stuffed our faces with divine warming curries, breads, popadoms and, of course, the hot chewy kebabs and roti breads that the Lahore is famous for. I have eaten kebabs the length and breadth of the country but still cannot find any to better the offering at the Lahore. We finished with mango lassi ice cream and left feeling like bloated pigs, returning home thoroughly satisfied.

Chapter Seven

If Sir Mark is unwilling to train me, there is at least one person I know who will take me on at 14 stone and shrinking: Charles Ralph Egerton, known to one and all as Edgy.

Edgy is a forty-five-year-old bachelor who runs Heads Farm, near Newbury, in Berkshire, the home of many famous racehorses, including the Cheltenham Champion Hurdle winner Mysilv, and Mely Moss, second in the 2000 Grand National. His winner-to-runner ratio is pretty good, too, and in three out of the previous eight seasons it had been better than any other trainer of National Hunt horses in the UK. He lives in a rambling 1930s house high up on the Berkshire Downs in the village of Chaddleworth. He is master of, if not all, a great deal of what he surveys. As well as his own house there is stabling for more than seventy horses, numerous houses, barns, a mechanical horse walker, offices, fields, paddocks, woodland and accommodation for the twenty-plus lads he employs. The house he now lives in is the one in which he was brought up and there are still pictures of the infant Charlie on the walls. It is a house that he says he never wants to leave, and this is where I shall make my home for the next three months.

Educated at Eton in the 1970s, Charlie is nevertheless not your typical upper-class Englishman. Horses are just one of his many passions, which include literature, music, politics and gardening. But his dominant passion is food, which is why it is such a pity that there is, as yet, no Mrs Edgy. We have much in common since he too is impetuous and unable to concentrate for long and loves his food, and we have shared many long evenings devouring food in his kitchen. He is devoted to his horses, and working with them is all that he has ever wanted to do. His schooling came to an abrupt end, around the time the teenage Edgy was called in by his bank manager in Eton. 'Now, young Egerton', he said, 'your overdraft is higher than my annual salary. What do you think I should do about that?' To which Charlie replied, 'Have you ever thought of getting a new job, sir.' The manager nearly conked out on the spot.

In late May, five months into my adventure, I packed my bags with a hard hat, some jodhpur boots, a pair of sheep shearer's jeans, numerous shirts, pullovers, undergarments and a wash bag. As I left the M4 at junction 14, I recalled that the last time we had met was at Goodwood races the previous summer, when he had been smoking like crazy. Although I had decided to try and quit again, I stopped at the petrol station in Great Shefford and bought a packet of cigarettes for Edgy. Healthwise this was not a great move. Charlie is a giant of a man, almost continually on a diet, and he suffers badly from asthma. There is something almost comic about the fact that he spends his life surrounded by midgets starving themselves all year round to make the weight to ride for their boss, and his idea of a diet is like that of no one I have ever met. It is all very well saying that you are going to live on cucumbers but Charlie's way of dealing with this would be to eat fifty a day to stave off the hunger pangs.

Manoeuvring the car through the large oak gates and down the gravel drive of Heads Farm that evening, I arrived in the kitchen just before eight o'clock waving the cigarettes at him. He looked up from the table and said, 'Oh, I've given up smoking but do go ahead yourself.' For the time being I resisted the temptation, but the longer I spent in the company of the stable lads the more I realized that smoking was going to be a great weapon for holding off the pangs of hunger I would have to put up with. For now, though, the cigarettes lay unopened on the kitchen table.

That evening we headed off for dinner at the Ibex Inn, a comfortable, old-fashioned pub down the lane from Heads Farm. We both ordered carrot and ginger soup, steak and salad and pints of water. When I say 'both' that is not the entire story because Charlie managed to sneak in two fried eggs and four bread rolls with butter while telling me that his dietician had expressly forbidden him to eat any bread. As he picked up the last roll he broke it in two and wiped it longingly around the inside of the butter dish, until every last smear had been dispatched from the dish onto the roll. In one movement, both roll and the butter disappeared. In the next breath, entirely oblivious of his crime, Charlie continued to tell me why he wasn't supposed to eat bread. It was crucial, he said, that he lose five stone and that fruit, grains and ginseng should now become the mainstays of his diet. I don't think for a minute that he knew what he was putting in his mouth as he said this.

We returned to Heads Farm, well fed and contented, where we drank a cup of black coffee topped up with a large slug of Pusser's rum before watching the news and retiring to bed. Horse people are up at first light, so bed before 10.30 p.m. is essential if you want to keep your wits about you.

I realized as I stripped off for bed and looked at myself in the bedroom mirror that it had been a long time since I'd been this weight. Even taking into account the couple of times I had fallen off the wagon since January, the clothes were looser, boxer shorts more comfortable, jeans easier to do up. And here I was in a wonderful, rambling house on the Berkshire Downs with horses all around me. I had been in training now for six months. Even though it had been an erratic combination of dieting, running, swimming and now riding, I had lost nearly two stone and I was on course to be fit and ready for the race day, a date for which had yet to be decided. I was so excited about finally riding out on the gallops that I had trouble getting to sleep, but tomorrow I had to get serious. Tomorrow would be my first day on a racehorse.

At 6 a.m., when Charlie banged on the door to wake me, I was already up and reading on my bed, fully dressed. 'You ready?' Charlie smiled, and I followed him downstairs.

That first morning I was introduced to Charlie's assistant trainer, Trigger, a smiling Irishman with an addiction to horses. Charlie said, 'Do exactly as Trigger says and he'll look after you.' Quite how he did this I will never know, because the moment we walked into the stables I realized that there was absolutely nothing that these sleek, trim, muscular horses had in common with the loveably plodding Daz. This was the business end of horse racing, and I must have been the least able jockey he had ever worked with.

Trigger's parents had had absolutely no interest in horses. His mother had been a nurse, and from an early age he had sought out the donkey down the road, and been inexplicably drawn to the horses in the fields near where he had grown up. Trigger made it clear that once he was out of short trousers there was nothing he wanted to do other than work with horses. Although he never said it, I imagined that one day he would be training horses out of his own stable.

After a tour of the stables, I sloped around Charlie's office as he took care of the morning's business. Pouring myself coffee, I picked up the equine directories from the shelves, and flicked through the stud books that are part and parcel of the everyday life of running a stable. Under a pile of paper, at first unseen, I glimpsed the corner of the 'Heads Farm Accident Book'. This I had not seen before.

The accident book is another weapon in the armoury of the Health and Safety Executive and every accident or fall that has taken place on the farm, no matter how minor, has to be recorded in it. Although a pointless document to most, I found it fascinating. I sat down and digested the following records from earlier in the year:

'Fell off banged head, X-rays taken. Horse jinked, fell, taken to Reading hospital fractured wrist, cast put on. It went crazy, bit finger. Horse slipped while being ridden knocked out tooth, went to dentist.'

'Horse spooked fell off. Picking out foot, she lashed out and kicked me, two broken bones in hand and broken wrist.'

'Horse reared over on top of me broken pelvis in 4 places and fracture in lower back.'

The last entry was even more terrifying because it had been written by Trigger, a man who was clearly one of the most capable ever to have sat on a horse.

Before I could read any further, Trigger was calling my name. I donned a jacket, some pigskin half-chaps, a helmet that my father would have approved of and walked out to the yard to jump up onto what Trigger called 'Pony'.

Pony was just that – Charlie's polo pony, and not a race-horse at all but a horse nevertheless. Although he looked like a miniature version of Daz, he was much more powerful and much speedier. But he was not exactly a flier, and I was a little disappointed since I had assumed that I would be stepping up to a real horse straight away. 'All in good time,' said Charlie. 'Let's watch you ride first, and then we'll see.' I resolved to prove that I was worthy of their precious time, and if I could keep out of the accident book that would be a bonus.

It was chilly and overcast in the yard as we all assembled beneath the whiteboard where, the night before, Charlie had written up which rider would be on what horse, how much each horse was to run and how many times it was going to be sent up the gallops. Some horses were racing fit and needed less work, others were brimming up to fitness but with no race to run, and some were coming back from injury, full of beans but not allowed strenuous work in case it impeded their recovery. Pony was down for one canter but I couldn't complain since a canter was still a steady gallop at almost a flat-out pace and was sure to test me to my limits.

The facilities at Heads Farm are laid out for routine. Everything at the farm is built around it since the horses love the regularity of their workout and the feeding. Oversleeping or being late is not something that happens in the horse world, and especially not in Trigger's world. In all my time at Heads Farm I was late only once and quickly got into the habit of setting my alarm for 5 a.m. to make sure it never happened again. Trigger's bollockings are rightly famous.

Trigger is a brilliant but firm teacher. You have to listen very carefully to him, though, because he doesn't say much, and I quickly learn to hang onto his every word. Trigger thinks that the best way to teach someone to race ride is to let them get on with it and get the feel of the horse. Once he was able to see how compatible I was with the horse then he could work out what I was doing wrong.

First off, I am thrown in at the deep end and given a very quick lesson about tacking up a racehorse. This is a very different proposition from tacking up a normal horse like Daz. For a start, the saddle isn't really a saddle at all; it's a piece of leather about the size of a handkerchief that you have to balance on. My first attempt does not go down well with Trigger. He is particularly unimpressed by the way I have put the saddle on. Without a word he walks into the stable, takes it, and the four pads lying underneath it, off Pony's back, and moves the saddle about two feet forward then tightens the girth straps.

I take Pony out into the yard where Albert, a former butcher from Mullingar, offers me a leg-up onto Pony's back. Only in his early forties, Albert needs a hip replacement, due, he thinks, to all the physical work, the riding and the cold, damp mornings. He has a hell of a limp but I've watched him flick up around fifteen lightweight lads onto their mounts. But with me being 14 stone, with little agility and no coordination, after a few disparaging remarks about my weight and one 'fuck that', he gives up and I clamber on using the mounting block.

In racing parlance a lad is a girl or boy who looks after the horses and tends to their needs. They ride them as the day breaks, muck them out and feed them. They are the crucial link between the horse and the trainer and a good lad is worth more than his weight in gold. Charlie has a lot of superb people working for him and he treats them well. The ones who work full-time for him are housed, have their council tax paid and receive a free subscription to Sky TV, so they can watch the racing (of course). They are paid around £300 a week before bonuses. But more than any financial remuneration, the real reward is being able to work so closely with the horses, and learning the fine art of turning a slow, wobbly two-year-old into a top-of-the-range, prize-winning machine. The ones who come simply to hunt for glory don't last long, and it is testament to Charlie's patronage that most of the lads have worked for him for years.

The lads who ride out with Trigger every morning at 6.30 are an eclectic mix. Predominantly they are Eastern Europeans who feed, water, muck out, nurture and cherish their charges, and are quite clearly the people who keep racing UK going. Then there is John, a cockney from Walworth, who tells me he always wanted to be a jockey, and has been a stable lad for more than thirty years. John's main passion is finding out what makes horses tick, and getting to grips with the psychology of their behaviour. He is one of the few people I have met who brings an intellectual curiosity to this world. He also rides like a dream and looks like he was born on the back of a horse. Significantly, at forty-seven he is exactly the same age as me.

Jason works for a firm of accountants and doubles up as a fitness trainer who rides between two and four lots every morning. He claims that he only does it for the petrol money and both he and John say they hate working with horses and would sooner do something else. I tell them I've done the 'something else' and that they don't know they've lived. The passion for horses that they have is something that never dies, and I don't believe for a minute that John and Jason really want to do anything else. Hanging in the back of Jason's car is the suit that he'll change into before heading to his day job, but you can see in his eyes that his heart is not really in it. This – fuelled by the intoxication of riding a horse at full speed – is where he really belongs.

Of them all, though, it is Josef who has the deepest understanding of the horses he works with. He lost his mother when he was fourteen and from then on he took solace in the horse. More than anything, he enjoys the challenge of winning over the really tricky horses, the ones that kick and bite. Sometimes it takes months to achieve this, but they all come around to Josef in the end. And when they do, he says, that is when he is most at peace with himself, and is unable to remove the glow of satisfaction from his face.

Josef told me how he would stand for hours in the stables just staring at his horses. In the past he was always given the really bad ones to look after, the juvenile delinquents, the horses that had a bad start in life and had been bashed around a bit. In the stables these were the horses that would rear up on top of you as you walked through the stable door, horses that bit and ones that kicked out if you turned your back on them. Josef has had his share of knocks but he keeps coming back to them with all his patience to try and coax them gently to be better behaved. With one particularly nasty horse he would stand at the end of its stable for hours on end, trying to coax it out of its corner. Over the days he would start to offer titbits in an outstretched hand and gradually the horse would relent. Slowly it would come forward and take the treat before darting back into the corner of its box. And Josef would repeat the exercise all over again until, finally, it would come forward and be calm enough to put its head in Josef's arms. It took months of persistence but Josef got it there in the end.

Then there's Penny who works as a racing secretary for the former Southampton and England centre forward Mick Channon, and Bianca, a pretty (but sometimes surly) lightweight Czech girl. A lot of her compatriots, like Josef, who had all his teeth knocked out by horses and doesn't trust British dentists so won't have them fixed, indicate that they would prefer to be frolicking with Bianca than with the horses, and they have a point.

Talking to them all as we amble to the gallops one thing becomes clear. They all want to ride in a race for Charlie. Although some of them have ridden in races – Eldiiar tells me he has won twelve in Kazakhstan, and Bianca says she has ridden and won races, too – the chances of that happening are about as likely as me winning mine. The reason is that all the Eastern Europeans who work for Charlie speak really bad English, and wouldn't be let anywhere near a race course since they would come a cropper with the required terminology. They understand lewd jokes but not much else, which is not a great help in the paddock. Charlie, ever the patrician Tory, has offered to pay for them to go to night school to improve their English but not one has taken up his offer. They are just obsessed with horses and horses can't talk, so why bother learning English?

The racing industry, like the rag trade, has always relied on this kind of migrant labour. Formerly trainers would enrol lads from the poorer parts of Glasgow, the East End of London and northern housing estates – all areas where malnutrition was high and the lads correspondingly small. Able to ride gigantic, often runaway speed-merchant horses with the minimum of interference with the horse's gait, pace and running ability, they have always been and remain the perfect athletes to guide the miscreant horse to the winning post. The lighter the weight on its back the faster the horse should run – that is the theory anyway. In practice it doesn't quite work out like that. Lester Piggott, possibly the most supremely talented of all latter-day jockeys, fought a constant battle with his weight and, standing at more than five feet nine inches, it was no surprise. There were just some horses that Lester couldn't ride because he was unable to make the weight; to starve and brutalize his body, spirit and mind was something that even he, the most competitive of all jockeys, could only go so far with. The same goes for Frankie Dettori, the contemporary equivalent of Piggott, who, with an irony that only the racing world fails to see, spends his spare time writing cookery books and some of his millions opening restaurants with 'celebrity chef' Marco Pierre White.

With improved nutrition, a growing welfare state and a National Health Service, short and stunted men have become very thin on the ground in the UK and Ireland. So trainers have started employing lads from India, Pakistan, Brazil and Eastern Europe. The average British male is now a stone heavier than he was twenty years ago. This, combined with the low pay for stable staff and the tendency for many more to remain in education beyond the age of sixteen, has caused a labour short-age and now more or less every yard in Lambourn and Newmarket has to rely on a welter of foreign labour. Lambourn trainer Jamie Osborne told me: 'It's very easy to get small riders – seven stone or just above – from abroad, but virtually impos-sible for a Briton to do that weight.' And when I interviewed former trainer Mark Pitman he told me, 'We have a mini United Nations here in Lambourn.' He calculated that 35 per cent of his workforce was made up of foreign nationals, and, what is more, he said that without exception they were all bril-liant. Certainly the young boys and girls I met at Lambourn all had that zest and zeal – the passion and irrational love – for the horses in their care. Because, although most of the immigrants are impoverished, there are much easier ways of earning a living, and a much better one, than looking after racehorses.

The horse-owning lot are, by and large, pretty right wing, and the natural inclination of those at the top of the ladder, including the trainers, is to disapprove of the immigrant hordes crushing into Britain. They have little truck with the nanny state or anything that smacks of socialism, class envy or a fairer distribution of the wealth of the nation. And little wonder. So much of what goes on in racing, particularly jump racing, goes directly back to the fox hunting field and, to top it all, it was a Labour government that banned hunting and forced through the dismemberment of horse racing's ruling elite, the Jockey Club. Until recently the Jockey Club was racings ruling body, now it is simply the landlord of racecourses, a ripe property company that might one day metamorphose into a harsh and uncaring commercial edifice. That would be sad, but is surely inevitable. Its disciplinary powers and prowess were gelded years ago, and today it is little more than a gentlemen's club – albeit a pretty agreeable one, with rooms in Newmarket where Englishmen can overimbibe and grunt and groan at the state of the nation and moan about the Labour Party – and who can blame them? There are one or two sporting Labour Party members of the house, notably Lord Donoughue, a keen owner and racing man, but for the most part they are a breed pretty much frowned upon by racing's elite and gilded class. These are men who remember when the adjective in Great Britain still meant something, mainly because their forebears helped make it that way. They have justifiable grouses and would prefer to see things carry on much as they did in the fifties and sixties. In the seventies the horror of horrors arrived, there was industrial unrest on their very doorstep.

Stable lads have always been paid a pittance, the unwritten trade-off being that what they don't get paid in cash they get by being able to work every day with animals they love and cherish. But things can only go so far and in the spring of 1975 industrial unrest came like a plague to Newmarket. Stable lads were then paid £28 per week, around £150 in today's money, and many complained that it was not enough to survive on. They took part-time jobs in the holidays, worked as cab drivers, painters and decorators, in fact did anything that would keep them where they wanted to be – with horses. The very rich men who owned them thought it an imposition that they actually wanted to earn enough money to subsist; surely the joy, the luxury and the all-embracing feel that the Thoroughbred can give you should be enough for these men and women who had, anyway, only ever known poverty of one sort or another?

The calamity hit the racing world when the stable lads went on strike just before the Guineas meeting in 1975. The lads were members of the TGWU union, led by a local organ-iser. As well as jockeys being pulled from horses on the Heath, the lads disrupted the Guineas meeting on the Saturday and then again on the Sunday when they stole a digger and dug up the Rowley Mile where the first Classic race of the season, the 2,000 Guineas, takes place. They were ultimately thwarted by a disgruntled group of race goers who hit out at the lads with their binoculars and rolled up copies of the *Sporting Life*. Class war had never been put under the microscope more pointedly. A pitched battle was narrowly avoided. Jockeys Lester Piggott and Willie Carson leapt to the rescue of the ruling elite by charging the lads on horseback. Carson, it should be said, later showed some remorse as he had once been a lad himself and said that, on balance, he was on the side of the underdog. He had a funny way of showing it. If at that point the jockeys had united with the lads there might have been real progress. But why would a jockey like Piggott, who, in the immortal words of Robert Sangster, was soon after being paid 'as much as Robert Redford', want to dirty his hands in defence of the lads, who every day readied his mounts and presented them to him in a gleaming, muscle-bound and pristine state so that he could win more races and fill up his bank accounts even more?

Gradually support for the strike faded and then went back to work. The main leaders left the industry or were fired, but finally owners realised that stable lads had to be paid a proper wage and the trainers would, as a result, would have to pass on the cost.

I remember striking lads pulling working lads off their horses on Newmarket Heath. It was very nasty and I had a great deal of sympathy for the workforce. You didn't need to be a lefty firebrand to realize that here were extremely rich men who were exploiting a fiscally poor and disadvantaged workforce for their own ends – so that they could get their horses trained on the cheap. The television news was full of images of the strike and I for one felt very sorry for them. While conditions have subsequently improved it cannot be said that stable lads now live in the lap of luxury, or, indeed, anywhere near it.

Stable lads are not in it for the cash; they're in it because they love the horse, the proud, strong beast that shows little emotion, that relies on man to be fed, watered and exercised, the animal that is so vulnerable yet can be so ferocious. Every lad of any standing that I have met has that feeling burning in his or her belly. For that reason, and that reason alone, the labour force that makes up horse racing the world over will for ever be shackled by its love of the horse. A sense of economic wellbeing doesn't come into it. Their principal complaints are the unsocial hours: early starts and late finishes. 40 years ago the job was easier with only two lots a day. But then the wages were a pittance. Now they have to work twice as hard, although the living standards have vastly improved.

The addiction grows stronger as lads age and, as they get older, they mellow and become less vociferous in their demands. They knuckle down and 'do' their two or three stables in the morning and then again in the evening. Some trainers take advantage of their employees who, like the heroin addict, come back time and time again for their equine fix. Every trainer in the world knows that they'll be back for more. Even the ones who get out of racing can never really shake it off. Ride out any morning from any training yard in the country and you will find warehousemen, taxi drivers, ex-jockeys with gnarled fingers and broken bones and even accountants, all riding horses for the love of it. They tell you that they only do it for a bit of spare cash or because times are hard, but scratch the surface and you discover that that is not the real story. They ride out because they love it, because the addiction and the passion are too strong. The pull of the horse is overwhelming, and I know and they know, and they know that I know, that there is nothing they can do about it. You might give it up, renounce it, flee from the demon, but in the end the horse always gets you, is always there with a welcoming nuzzle or whinny, will always bring you back into its embrace.

Every single lad who goes into racing, often malnourished and with a limited education, dreams of riding that Derby winner, thinks and dares to believe that greatness will come his way. As in professional football it rarely works out like that, and even for those who do achieve it, greatness can come at a price. Racing's top tier is littered with bulimics, drug abusers, alcoholics and people who can't quite relate to the world they live in. The greatest jockey of the nineteenth century, Fred Archer, not only battled with his weight but he fought a battle with what today would be recognized as mental illness. Every trainer and every owner in the land wanted to employ the services of Archer. He was a national hero and newspapers filled their columns with stories about him. He won races that no other jockey could, he was feted and lauded and loved by the racing world and the public. Yet he was besieged by depression that tormented him until he could take no more. At five foot ten, battling his weight and aged just twenty-nine, at the pinnacle of his power but in a fit of delirium he loaded a revolver and shot himself dead. The revolver and Archer's silks are still on display at the National Racing Museum in Newmarket. It is a vivid reminder of a tragedy that continues to play itself out, even today, albeit not in so dramatic or stark a fashion.

There is an additional factor. Smoking is a great appetite suppressant and that is what all jockeys need – something to kill the constant pangs, the aches, the rage and the sheer monotony of not eating, and a lot of jockeys smoke. Lester Piggott worked his way through cigars, Pat Eddery was a regular twenty-a-day man, and in a gesture of defiance against political correctness a lot of yards allow the lads to smoke their heads off. Cleaning tack, shovelling shit and riding out on the gallops, there is nearly always a blue plume in the air above the heads of many of the lads. I've never seen a trainer tell a lad to put out a cigarette. Racing is the last bastion of the ever so polite fuck you culture and I think in some small way that is yet another reason I love it so much.

Others who might not smoke turn to diuretic pills, many induce vomiting and yet others take Class A drugs. Cocaine and amphetamine abuse is very much a fact of life in the racing towns of Newmarket and Lambourn. Performance-enhancing drugs are not difficult to get hold of in either place.

The former champion jockey Kieren Fallon, as good an exponent of the art of race riding as there has been in the last twenty years is, as I write, still serving out the last part of an eighteen-month ban for cocaine abuse and is under constant psychiatric care. In a remarkably frank and lucid interview with Jim McGrath in the *Daily Telegraph*, published on 13 August 2009, Fallon, said: 'Outside riding, I find life a little more difficult. Meeting people … in situations. When I'm on a horse, it's completely different. Nothing bothers me. Whereas, I feel uncomfortable around different people.'

*   *   *

As we descend towards the gallops the banter among the lads is about football and racing their horses and, of course, Charlie, 'the guv'nor'. There is no sparing the blushes for the girls and the air is full of expletives: 'He's a right cunt, a right fucker, he is,' one says, talking about his least favourite footballer. 'You're right, he's a cunt,' says another. Yet another chips in: 'He's a double fucking cunt for the way he gave that penalty away, John.' The conjugation of words reminds me of the wonderful Peter Cook and Dudley Moore sketches in the 1970s in which the pair did a spoof horse race commentary from Newmarket called 'At The Races', where each horse was named either after a sexual organ, a body part or a general sexual innuendo. The girls don't even notice, the lads don't baulk. They talk kindly to their mounts, as though pretending to pose for the cameras as they stand in the stirrups high above the withers. Trigger barks the orders and they settle down again. There is a job to be done after all.

We get to the bottom of the hill and then trot along parallel to the road on the other side of the hedge. We cross the road, another small field to another road crossing and then across another mile or so to the foot of the gallops. As we circle and swing round right-handed, I can feel Pony give a pull and a leap forward, but he doesn't seem as if he's going to run off. I feel well balanced and confident enough to give him a squeeze and then we are off, shooting up the half-mile hill, puffing and blowing and pulling a little. I stroke his neck and rub his mane and ask him to look after me. I tell him that I haven't done this for ages and when I last did it I wasn't much good. Halfway up and he pulls a bit more. He's keen and wants his head but in front there's a horse that I mustn't overtake. The wet sand and rubber that makes up the all-weather track spits up into my face and eyes and splatters down his front. I try and edge myself into a position more in keeping with a jockey than a sack of potatoes but my stirrups are too long. Pony takes a huge gulp of air, and in the last half-furlong I let him have his head. He slows; puffing and blowing, the pair of us grind down to a trot, then a walk. The sweat pours off him, his muzzle drips with the salted fluid that swells up in beads and bursts dripping to the ground. For six months this is what I have been waiting for, and it is magical.

Chapter Eight

Quite apart from having to lose weight, and learning how to ride a proper horse, there were some issues over which I had no control. Under Jockey Club rules you cannot ride wearing spectacles. As I've been short-sighted since my late teens, one spring afternoon I cycled over to Moorfields Eye Hospital to weigh up the pros and cons of having my eyes lasered. The surgeon I was booked in to see had taken care of jockeys in the past and told me that the process was simple and 'only costs £2,000 an eye'. My passion was becoming very expensive indeed. I asked what the chance of failure was. 'One in ten thousand,' he replied. But when I ask how he defined failure, he replied, 'You go blind.' I made my excuses and left.

Later that day I asked my mother for her advice. After psychology and communism, teaching and socialism she went to work at the Department of Health. It had been her job to evaluate and allocate government research money for exactly this kind of thing. 'Don't do it,' she advised. She said that the operation was still in its infancy and there was still a chance that it could go wrong. I was going to have to ride without glasses, but was comforted by the knowledge that many jockeys do exactly the same thing.

The British Racing School at Newmarket has more or less taken the place of the old apprentice scheme where a lad would be apprenticed to a trainer to learn how to ride properly. It is run by an ex-military man called Rory MacDonald and is partly funded by central government and partly by the racing industry itself. If you want to learn to become a jockey it is *the* place to go.

One day in mid-May, therefore, now hitting a sprightly 13½ stone, I took myself off to meet MacDonald, a forthright individual but one who, nevertheless, has the interests of the racing industry, and particularly the welfare of apprentice jockeys, at heart. 'The average wage in East Anglia is £19,000, the average wage of a stable lad is £14,000,' he told me rather sternly. I pressed him on this anomaly. After all, the owners who ultimately fund racing are hugely rich; didn't he think that it was, at the very least, disingenuous and, at worst, extremely mean-spirited that they didn't contribute more? MacDonald is far too much of a diplomat to give me a straight answer, but he cares deeply for the waifs and strays who turn up with dreams in their heads of becoming champion jockeys, and it was what he *didn't* say that really spoke volumes. He didn't – perhaps couldn't – defend the industry.

I told MacDonald my story and he agreed to take me on. He introduced me to former jockey Richard Perham and to a former army PT instructor called Ian Holt who had followed MacDonald out of the army to the British Racing School. The plan was that I'd drive to Newmarket every other week and have a two- or three-hour training session on a mechanical horse to work on my technique.

First they wanted to find out how fit I was. I was asked to change into a sweatsuit and trainers and then made to do press-ups, sit-ups, hop, skip and jump and something to do with a bench that I couldn't quite fathom. The sweatsuit was soaked through, muscles ached, my heart raced and exhaustion crept up on me and, after an hour, all I wanted to do was go home. These were proper, old-fashioned British Army training exercises that I was being put through and it hurt, both physically and emotionally. When I was finished I was told to buy a new pair of trainers and a heart-rate monitor to keep a record of my fitness progress. The initial assessment was that I'd be a marginal case for getting a jockey's licence.

I spent the summer driving back and forth to Newmarket, and gradually improved my fitness and technique. Of all the time I spent there, the most fantastic moment came when I watched what seemed like an entire generation of teenagers arrive, all of whom were dying to get into the horse racing world and harboured dreams of being the next Frankie Dettori or AP McCoy. Some had been sent because they'd expressed an interest, others because they were small and undernourished, and their schools careers' advisers thought that riding a horse was the only chance they had of a fulfilling professional career. I stood and watched, really rather blinded by them all as they laughed and pushed and jostled down the utilitarian corridors of the BRS. They reminded me of the corridors of Witney Agricultural College where I had harboured the same kind of dreams all those years before.

After a morning in the sweatsuit I thought I would be sent on my way, but before I had a chance to catch my breath I was instructed to get changed. It was time to ride the mechanical horse.

Richard Perham rode more than two hundred winners and was a superb teacher. Lesson number one was all about how the jockey should sit on the horse. I was told I had to imagine posing in the shape of a cocktail glass, head, elbows and heels all in a vertical line. Before long he had me cantering on the mechanical horse and then galloping in front of a large video screen showing an actual race filmed from the jockey's perspective. He also filmed my efforts at staying on his engineered beast as I clung on for dear life, heart palpitating, legs aching and burning with pain. At the end of the first day I was so exhausted that I sort of fell off the machine in a rather undignified manner before we sat down and talked in more depth about the details that I would need to consider before I got to race day. One of the issues that I would have to deal with was handicapping, which was introduced into certain races with the aim that every horse should cross the finishing line at the same time.

In order to make the race more challenging there are races in which each horse is handicapped by additional weight, decided, according to a horse's ability, by the official handicapper. The faster the horse runs on one day, the more weight it is required to carry in subsequent races. If a horse runs badly in a following race it will be given less weight to carry. For Sir Mark Prescott and thousands of trainers around the world this is the greatest challenge of all, since the aim is to outwit the handicapper and slip your horse under his radar on the big day. To do this the trainer needs to get the horse constantly to improve from its previous race, or, indeed, to regress from its last performance in order to qualify for lighter weights the next time out. Every horse crossing the finishing line at the same time makes for a fairer race – that is the theory, in practice it has never happened, and probably never will. It is a system that, due to the inherent gambling element in racing, is rife with conflict, machinations and skulduggery.

The greatest of all turf administrators, Admiral Henry John Rous (1795–1877), who, as well as being a steward of the sport's then ruling body, the Jockey Club, was also its official handicapper, wrote: 'Every great handicap offers a premium to fraud, for horses are constantly started without any intention of winning, merely to hoodwink the handicapper.'

In handicapping horses by weight, Rous's objective was to get every horse in the race to cross the line at the same time, something that more than two hundred years after his death has still not been achieved. There are occasional dead heats with two, sometimes three, horses passing the finishing post at the same time but never in the history of racing has an entire field crossed the line together.

Rous used to attend every major race meeting with a huge nautical telescope, a relic of his seafaring days, which he would position strategically in the grandstand. Immediately following the race he would hurry down to see which horses were blowing hardest, and assessed their strengths and weaknesses, making detailed notes as he did so.

Rous established that each pound in weight was equivalent to a horse's length. So if horse A beat horse B by seven lengths then the next time they met horse A would be handicapped by an additional seven pounds, and so on through the ranks of the field. What Rous could not take into account were the machinations and double-dealing of the trainer and the jockey. There were also other considerations, with younger, and less experienced, horses being given less weight. It is a testament to Rous's skill that, even after two hundred years, the scientific method that he devised is still the benchmark used today.

*   *   *

With four months to go until the race I still had more than half a stone to lose. While 12 stone was the weight I assumed, back in January, that I had to get myself down to, in reality it needed to be less than this to take into account the additional weight of the saddle, helmet and all the riding kit that would be factored in when I stood in the weighing-in room just before the race. Any additional weight would hamper my chances and slow the horse down, and it was imperative that I gave the horse the best possible chance of carrying me around the entire course. 'Do everything I tell you and you'll be all right,' Perham said as I left the training room that first day. Between the mechanical horse and Heads Farm, they were going to forge a jockey out of me, no matter how much pain it involved.

Chapter Nine

Back at Heads Farm, against all the advice I was given, I start jogging twice a day, up and down the track to the village. I stick to my salads, beans and pulses, while Charlie feigns adherence to his diet. One morning I come down to breakfast to find twelve cooked sausages with as many rashers of bacon laid out on the kitchen table with fried eggs. I assume they are for the stable lads until Charlie pulls out a single plate and a knife and fork and starts tucking in all by himself. This has been cooked for him by Pam, his housekeeper, and is supposed to be for some visiting owners. They will be very lucky indeed if they get anything at all.

Each morning I am up, as usual, before six, waiting for Trigger to instruct me before we head out to the gallops. After riding two, sometimes three horses, at around eleven I return to the house and plunge into as hot a bath as I can run, topping it up from the hot tap as the water cools. For twenty minutes I lie there sweating, getting more and more dizzy as the heat burns out of me, before clambering out and lying on the bath mat to regain my composure, tiny silvery stars appearing in my vision. Getting to my knees, drained, dehydrated and exhausted, I climb into bed and sleep until lunchtime. This is the daily life of the jockey, and if I am serious about joining their ranks I must do as they do.

The most important development of the summer was that I had started smoking again. Along with the riding, the running, the baths and the diet, this had a dramatic impact on my weight loss. This was not because it directly helped me lose weight, but it took my mind off food, and smothered my appetite between the plates of food that now passed as my meals.

One of the greatest smokers of all time was my friend Jonathan Cooper, who used to lurk on the steps of the Express Newspapers building, where I was City editor of the *Sunday Express* and he was a feature writer on the *Daily Express*. With a crumpled pack of Rothmans we used to pass the time talking about the next race and the 'big one' that was going to underwrite every previous betting loss.

The entire Cooper clan have the horse bug. Their late father, Tom, was a bloodstock agent and widely considered to be the best spotter of a champion racehorse of his generation. Jonathan's mother, Valerie, owned a very good jumping mare called Opera Hat. Although I never brought it up with him directly, I often wonder what would have happened if I'd been born into Jonathan's world.

On the office steps or in the betting shop we talked endlessly about horses, the excitement brewing as we got closer to the most important date in our racing calendar – the Cheltenham Festival. Every year in March we would board a train for the festival, where Jonathan would leave me out in the rain while he went to have lunch with a bookmaker and shared tips on the forthcoming season. He knew who was paying and he would laugh like mad when he returned, seeing my collar turned up against the weather, as I waited impatiently for the latest insider gossip.

Linus, Jonathan's youngest, was just six months old when the call came through to our Dorset cottage. It was a dark Saturday evening, cold, and the wood burner was roaring. 'I'm very sorry,' the caller, a mutual friend, said, 'but Jonathan died this afternoon.' Jonathan dropped dead on a Saturday afternoon in the hallway of his home in London without any warning. Since he had packed in the cigarettes, some years before, and had started going to the gym, there was nothing in his lifestyle or what he ate or drank that indicated that this was going to happen.

While he had been epileptic, what actually killed Jonathan was an ulcer that ruptured an artery. His wife, the ambulance men, his sister-in-law, who was a doctor, and the hospital all tried to save him but it was hopeless. He'd been to the cinema to see an early showing of the recently released film about Seabiscuit, the American wonder horse that captured that nation's imagination. He came home, drank some wine, ate some lunch and collapsed.

I don't think any death, except that of my father, has ever affected me so badly, and the shock was overwhelming. Jonathan was buried next to his father at a church in Monasterevin, his hometown in Co. Kildare, on a very dark and chilly November day in 2003. I was a pallbearer, and the undertaker made us laugh with his jokes about the weight of the coffin and the distance to Jonathan's resting place. The church was packed with people who had flown in from London and everyone in Ireland who had anything to do with the Thoroughbred racehorse was there. John Magnier, the godfather of horse racing, turned up to pay his respects, took a pew in the balcony and kept his head down and his emotions in check.

On the afternoon of the funeral, tanked up with drink, I suggested to Jonathan's mother that we should organize a horse race in Jonathan's memory. She thought it was a grand idea. 'If you do he'll be looking down on us having a little punt. He used to love gambling on handicap races,' she said.

As the idea formed, friends and family handed over large sums of money in their droves, and the Jonathan Cooper Memorial Stakes was born, run once at Sandown and once at Epsom. The third occasion of the race, in July 2007, was interrupted by the London underground bombing and the following year we had a party in Ireland instead, at Jonathan's brother's house. It was later in Ireland, while staying with his brother Patrick, that I got to know about a horse that had the potential to change a lot of lives. A horse called Curtain Call.

It is something that happens so very rarely in racing but in the spring and early summer of 2008 the magic wand of luck was about to wave itself across the shoulders of the three lucky owners of one brilliant horse, Curtain Call. Throughout the season it had done absolutely everything right and was all set to win the greatest racing show on earth, the Epsom Derby.

Curtain Call was a small, thick-set, stroppy bay that had set all the newspapers and half of Newmarket alight with dreams. In a rare moment of misjudgement, John Magnier had missed a golden opportunity when he was put up for sale eighteen months earlier. That horse, which had trained well, eaten well and shown all the precociousness of a genius in the making, was about to be tested, and it was sent from Ireland to be trained in Newmarket by Luca Cumani, who had handled two previous Derby winners, to give it the best possible chance. As the big day approached I would drive more and more frequently to Newmarket to watch horse and trainer out on the gallops and to marvel at the beauty of this rough diamond.

The children were beside themselves with excitement, too, and at breakfast each morning we scoured the papers for reports on the horse and collected articles that tipped it to be that year's winner. It was the first time that we had felt so closely involved in something so big, and while we adults started to talk about how much we would wager on the day, the children decided how much pocket money they wanted to set aside for the horse. It is so rare to be involved with a potential wonder horse and even though we were on the periphery we had already started to invest hard cash in the outcome. The owners had already started putting wagers down too, resulting in the odds being shortened considerably as race day approached. With that his value rocketed – a clever move by the owners.

A year before he arrived in Newmarket, Curtain Call had been worth just 60,000 guineas. He was now valued at £3.75 million. Eager to hedge their bets, the trio then decided to sell shares in him at £75,000 each, but this was an investment strictly for the bloodstock professionals. And that is what the original owners were. Jimmy George, a director of the blood-stock auction house, Tattersalls, Bill Oppenheim, an American who brings a rare intellect to the business of breeding the racehorse and Patrick Cooper, Jonathan's brother and a bloodstock agent of high repute. Further investments were made by breeders and owners eager to jump on the band-wagon. After he'd won the Derby, Curtain Call would then be worth around £20 million. He had a good bloodline, having sprung from the loins of Sadler's Wells, one of the most successful stallions of all time when it came to siring winners. Everyone would be cashing in.

While other Derby contenders raced at Lingfield Park Derby trial a month or so before the race, Curtain Call was taken to Nottingham for a not too difficult preparatory race against two other Derby rivals. He won at a stroll, and the tension mounted. Curtain Call fever had arrived.

For race day Rose prepared the most delicious Derby Day picnic for everyone involved. The whole family, along with our au pair, Pauline, decamped to Epsom for the day, the children and Pauline getting terribly excited because the Queen was going to be there.

For the London contingent a luxury minibus had been hired that would leave from Pimlico at 10 a.m. prompt – only it didn't because the driver got the wrong address and it was 10.30 before we left, all besuited and bejewelled in top hats and tails, with shimmering rocks on fingers and pearls round the neck. We were doing all this, not just for our three friends who owned Curtain Call, but to worship the horse that was going to win the Derby. That was what our trip was really all about: a homage to the horse.

I had last been to Epsom Downs for Jonathan's memorial race, and I raised a glass to him as we passed through the gates of the racecourse. As we pulled into the car park we could already scent victory and we begun unpacking the feast and uncorking champagne and wine that had been brought in a separate vehicle by Rose. Half an hour before the race I wandered off in a haze of alcoholic inebriation to plunder more money on Curtain Call. He had been tipped in several of the morning papers and his price had shortened again considerably. After procuring a press badge I was able to enter the area where the jockeys congregate. There were my heroes all full of adrenalin and nerves, on edge before the big race, the only race that *really* matters. Tiny, half-starved boys and men, all with a longing, a desire, to win this one race, the biggest of the year. Tomorrow they would be back chasing bad no-hopers around Lingfield Park or Wolverhampton, or anywhere else they were asked (or in some cases told) to go. I tried to think about what must have been going through their minds in these last minutes of preparation as they calmly went about making the final checks and getting last instructions from their trainers. I could feel my palms getting sweaty just at the thought of what was about to happen. This was as nervous as I had ever been before any race, and I wasn't even on a horse.

Looking at the gaunt faces of the jockeys and their frail looking bodies, I sucked in my girth and imagined what it would be like to be one of them. I kept asking myself why they did it. But I knew the answer. It was because of the glory that beckoned, the danger, the defiance of death.

Earlier in the day the wife of one of the owners of Curtain Call had said to me that owning a horse like him was potentially life-changing. 'You do know that if he wins today we will never ever have to worry about money again.' There was so much resting on this one horse, for so many, that it was difficult, through the alcohol, not to get overly sentimental. With ten minutes to the off we wandered, rather unsteadily, up to the grandstand as the horses readied at the start line. 'He can do it, I know he can do it,' I heard someone say behind me. I lit a cigarette and started chewing my nails in heady anticipation. In little over two minutes our three friends would either be millionaires many times over or very, very disappointed.

It took an age for the horses to be loaded into the starting stalls, but finally they were off and they quickly spread out all over the course. The minute jockeys on top of these bold, ferocious beasts needed to conserve the energy of their mounts as much as possible. At the same time they had to get into a good position so that they weren't boxed in and unable to break free. They had to weigh up the option of taking the inside rail, thereby travelling a shorter distance, or getting on the outside, where they could run free and clear. All the while they needed to stay alert to the moment when they would give the horse a kick, indicating that now was the time to storm down the hill to the finishing line.

Whatever decision the jockey makes, there is always a certain amount of jostling and hustling that passes unnoticed by the punters. There is also a good deal of shouting and swearing that goes on with jockeys refusing to give ground, while they look for a gap to slip through, as their weakened bodies all but give up on them.

Somewhere in the middle of the melee was our jockey, Jamie Spencer, clinging on for dear life as the horses bumped each other and turned for the final straight. We all knew that he had been told to swing wide as they got to the top of the hill before unleashing Curtain Call with such a blistering turn of pace that all the other horses will be left in his wake.

Only he didn't.

As we saw them round Tattenham Corner on their descent towards the winning post we knew there was trouble. Curtain Call was boxed in and well back in the field. Jockey Spencer was not covering himself in glory. He had hardly been mentioned in the running commentary but we were shrieking and screaming and the whole of Epsom Downs was alight with the roar of the crowd. But he was in terrible trouble, with nowhere to go, and as Sheikh Mohammed's (or, to be precise, his wife, Princess Haya's) horse, New Approach, stormed to victory Curtain Call and Spencer were nowhere to be seen.

He came tenth. It was a victory of sorts for the Ruler of Dubai. Not perhaps the ultimate accolade of the horse winning in his own colours but a victory for the family, and the man who had spent tens of billions on horses in the hope of winning this one race. Trainer Cumani stormed off back to Newmarket in a huff, complaining bitterly about the ride the jockey had given his horse. The mood in the car park as we gathered to drown our sorrows was sombre and sanguine. Jimmy said, 'That's racing'; Patrick chipped in with 'We live to fight another day'. But the best comment came from Fiona Mahony, whose quiet, shy, self-deprecating husband is chairman of Tattersalls, where Jimmy George has his day job as marketing director. She turned to me and said, 'Oh, well, it appears that we won't need to be advertising for a new marketing director … just yet.' The dream was well and truly shattered, but worse was to come.

While Sheikh Mohammed, Princess Haya and their entourage boarded their helicopter bound for Newmarket, a group of us clambered onto the minibus that Patrick had laid on for the trip back to London, I left Rose, Pauline and the children to their own devices and they made their way back in the car that had ferried the lavish picnic to Epsom Downs. Weary, exhausted and still drowning our sorrows, I was dropped off – or, rather, shoved out of – the bus on the south side of Battersea Bridge and staggered merrily home with the sound of 'Do you think he'll be all right? Shouldn't we drop him at his door?' wafting from the interior of the bus.

Curtain Call never did reach his full potential. He was so well bred that there was a chance he might make a good sire, and with it hundreds of millions of pounds for his owners. But for Curtain Call, the winner of more than £200,000, it was not to be. He subsequently ran in a race at Kempton Park where the purse was generous and the hopes high once again. But on that track, a little more than a year after his Derby disaster, Curtain Call met his maker. Another horse crashed into the bottom half of a hind leg, severing all the tendons. He was destroyed on the spot.

Chapter Ten

By midsummer I was coming down to Heads Farm to train twice, sometimes three times a week, and settling into a proper routine. One afternoon I ventured to the town of Wantage, where there was a gruesome little market in the square. A couple of East End wide boys were selling fruit, an Asian man was trading shell suits and trainers and a pretty girl with sallow skin was working at a fish stall. I bought some anchovies, smoked salmon and skate wings in the hope of getting Charlie back onto something resembling a diet. Returning to Heads Farm, we sat down to watch the 6.20 at Kempton Park, where Charlie had a runner, Smooth As Silk, on the all-weather track, before I set about cooking the skate wings, which we ate with capers and salad.

I had come across Smooth As Silk before in the yard. She was a neurotic slip of a thing who had all but chewed her way out of her box with her crib-biting, and was prone to wind sucking as well. Although when she arrived at the stables she had shown some promise she looked to me about as likely to become a racehorse as Charlie did to becoming a jockey. If she were a human she'd talk at a rate of knots, chain-smoke and, in all likelihood, be anorexic, too. The race proved to be disastrous. Starting at odds of 25-1, the bookmakers once again proved that they were not being overly pessimistic. She came last.

Charlie may be many things but he isn't a bullshitter. The Hankinsons, who made their money from concrete and have spent at least £1 million of it buying racehorses for Charlie to train, are telephoned immediately. He offers no excuses. 'Some horses are just useless, they maybe show a lot of promise but then they are not right in the head,' he offers by way of explanation. The Hankinsons take it well, but Charlie is feeling very low. He has trained two winners for the family. They have shown great faith in him, but somehow it is just not going right. For years Charlie has had a brilliant strike rate of winners to runners but recently this has dropped to the near-industry average of around 10 per cent.

The trainer's life is a precarious one. Many go broke or run into serious financial problems, with many issues taken out of their hands. Owners don't pay, horses go lame and from time to time a horse has to be put down. Some jockeys, often without the trainer knowing, also have unhealthy relationships with bookmakers and professional gamblers. Graham Bradley, a very talented jockey who won just about every race in his chosen discipline of jumping, used to fix races regularly on behalf of a cocaine trafficker and career criminal called Brian Wright. Bradley was warned off by the Jockey Club, who regulated the sport, for eight years, and banned from having anything to do with racing or racehorses ever again. In 2007, Wright was sentenced to thirty years in prison for importing cocaine, the proceeds of which he used to launder through racing. It was alleged at the time that Wright had corrupted an entire generation of jockeys. Most surprising, and in a strange way upsetting, to me was the manner in which his fellow jockeys leapt to Bradley's defence. It was depressing to read of a whole raft of top-class jockeys, including the great AP McCoy, giving evidence on behalf of Bradley, who did more damage to racing than any other individual in a generation.

It is this type of behaviour that will ultimately be to the detriment of the trainer and his business. Stable lads, many from poor backgrounds, misbehave and get into punch-ups. Drink and drug abuse in Newmarket is higher than in many other market towns as young lads battle with the stress of the job and often with their weight. The trainer has to deal with all of that, too. For the successful ones the rewards are great. Top-flight trainers such as Aidan O'Brien or Sir Michael Stoute are millionaires many times over. For the others it is a hand-to-mouth existence.

The trainer has to assess the horses in his yard and then supervise the breaking in. Then he has to get them to accept a saddle and bridle and a man on their back and, above all, to go forward, to keep going forward and to remain doing that willingly in each of the four gaits, walk, trot, canter and gallop. He has to weigh them, feed them and get them fit for racing. He has to try and ensure that their mental health is up to being trained in order to win races. Not only must the horse be physically fit, it must also be mentally agile and tough.

The upside is that horse racing is an industry that demands to be fed with new stock. As a result there is a vast, worldwide breeding operation in which horses are flown all over the world to be mated with other horses in the hope of breeding that elusive champion. It is an expensive business for all concerned, and it is the perfect way to burn through a newly made fortune. However, if you do want to breed a winning racehorse, there is one person, above all others, you should turn to: the Irishman John Magnier, the leader of the so-called Coolmore Mafia. This is a group of very rich racehorse owners who, from time to time, congregate in Fethard, Co. Tipperary, the headquarters of the Coolmore Stud. The most visible are Derrick Smith, a former employee of Ladbrokes, Michael Tabor, a former bookie, Dermot Desmond, a stockbroker and financier, and J. P. McManus, a former tipper truck driver and bookie. All are affiliates of Magnier and revel in their roles on and off the racecourse, swaggering around the paddock, knowing that the world is watching them. They know that when they arrive at a racetrack or a horse auction the tempo rises, people nudge each other and point knowingly in their direction. When Magnier goes to work in the auction ring he brings a hushed silence to the floor as he bids millions for the next horse he thinks will win all the garlands and then go on to sire or foal another champion racehorse. The group enjoy the limelight, but they rarely give interviews and never about their business interests. Magnier might mumble a few sage words for the television cameras in his Tipperary brogue about the merits of a particular horse he owns, but there is a great deal about the intricacies of the Coolmore empire that is off-limits. There are offshoots of Coolmore in the USA and Australia, and it is quite simply the most successful stallion farm in the world. Time and again Coolmore stallions top the league table of champions all over the world. If you can get into the club, it is a fantastic place to be.

For an outsider, the best position to be in the industry is as a seller of bloodstock. It is entirely unregulated, with no commission in charge of ensuring transparency in the marketplace. Unlike most other forms of auction it is perfectly legal to bid for your own horse. This can be pretty handy if you have inside information about how much someone else might pay for a horse, particularly if it is yours that is being sold, or if there is an agent involved who might convince a client that a particular young, unbroken colt or filly has a million pounds worth of potential whereas in reality it has about seventeen shillings and sixpence worth. The vendor, agents and auctioneer will all say that nobody forced anybody to buy a horse and that the true value of an animal can be ascertained in the auction ring, but that is surely missing the point.

This is the world that Charlie has to deal with on a daily basis, and when he is not on hand at the stables looking after his latest charges it means that he is standing in another auction ring with a client looking to pick out his next winner. While he is away Trigger is in charge, and during the summer, while Charlie was absent for long stretches at a time, I learnt a great deal about the man who runs his lads on a very short leash.

What becomes immediately clear about Trigger is that he has eyes in the back of his head. One morning Eldiiar, who has a tendency really to hammer the horses going up the gallops, even when given specific instructions not to, let one of the horses fly when he thought Trigger wasn't looking. I was behind him and could see what he was doing; Trigger was in front and couldn't. Or that's what I thought and certainly what Eldiiar thought. He was in for quite a shock when he got to the crest of the gallop. Looking down at the tranquil, quiet horizon with birds singing and hares tearing around, the silence was broken by Trigger bawling at Eldiiar: 'That'll be the last time you ever do that, you little fucker, how dare you chase after him, he's not a machine. You've knocked him back in his training by weeks,' bellowed Trigger.

By any standards it was a ferocious bollocking and a deserved one. How Trigger had seen what Eldiiar was up to I will never know. I could only put it down to experience and some phenomenally accurate calculator in his head since he knows almost exactly how long it takes each horse at a particular pace to get to the top of the gallop. If one gets there ahead of the time he has calculated in his head, it has done one of two things. Either the horse has run away with the jockey or the jockey has geed up the horse to lengthen its pace. Eldiiar stared at his feet while Trigger bollocked him, but I understood why he did it: it was for that rush of adrenalin that he, I and all the rest of the lads are here for in the first place. From time to time they forget that they are here to do a job for Trigger and Charlie as well.

Since many of the lads have aspirations to become real jockeys, when a professional comes to visit Charlie to put one of his horses through its paces so that he can establish its progress and work out which race they should be aiming for, the lads are all ears. When one of the greats arrives at the gallops it is the only time they fall silent, hoping to pick up tips as to how they, too, might one day ride the big race.

Losing close to three stone, as I have by now done, is one of the hardest things I have ever achieved, but this is nothing compared to the routine that real jockeys endure on a daily, weekly, annual basis. Shane Kelly, a regular visitor to Charlie's stables, is just one of hundreds of up-and-coming jockeys who are vying for that one moment of glory. At first he was reluctant and a little embarrassed to talk about it, but when I pushed a bit harder he talked me through the unbelievably gruelling routine that he lives by, seven days a week, from his base in Newmarket.

'I have a spoonful of porridge for breakfast which is followed by a two-mile run, quite often in the dark. After that I ride out two, maybe three horses for whichever of the Newmarket trainers has booked me to ride. Then I get in the car and I am sent to the racetrack. I'm usually driven by my father-in-law in order to conserve energy. Little sips of water are taken during the day and for lunch I have a boiled sweet. The sugar gives me some oomph.'

Kelly is just another ordinary jockey and on race day will ride between two and eight races. The better he gets the more popular he will become and the more rides he will secure. After a day of racing he will sometimes head off for an evening meeting where he might ride another six horses. He's lucky if he gets back to Newmarket by midnight and he's up at five the following morning to do it all over again.

I am now completely dedicated to training my mind, although while I am resting I often wonder what harm just one decent blow-out, like in the good old days, could do. When this happens, all I have to do to steady my nerves is to remind myself what these jockeys go through on a daily basis and see that there is no comparison between what I am doing and what they do month in month out. I think if I tried, even for a couple of days, to follow Kelly's diet I would probably expire.

My teacher and mentor, Richard Perham, who I go to see regularly at the British Racing School, is amazed there aren't more traffic accidents involving jockeys.

'The exhaustion is the thing that gets to you, the constant wasting, the pain, the hours and hours of eating nothing but a bit of lettuce and a piece of white fish. It all takes its toll. Constant miles driving from home to a trainer to test the skills of a particular horse then onto a race meeting and then another race meeting and then home and bed and the same thing starts all over again the following morning. All I wanted to do was be a jockey. I succeeded but in the end I just couldn't take it any more. I couldn't do the weight and I couldn't do the starvation.'

It is Richard's words that I repeat to myself when I feel I am about to waver. To fulfil my dream requires only a small sacrifice in comparison to what these lads have to put themselves through.

Perham, too, was brutalized during his racing career. Booked to ride a no-hoper for one of the country's top trainers, and aware that the ride could be the start of something better, he took a tumble just before the race and heard the sound of his ankle snapping. In agony, he could only think about getting to hospital and having the leg fixed. The trainer had other ideas, as Perham recalls. 'He said to me, "Get back on that fucking horse and ride it, if you don't you'll never ride for me again." So I got back on, the pain was excruciating, unbearable, and I gave the horse a shit ride, but I did get other rides from the trainer, which is exactly what I wanted.'

Starvation diets, like many other things in racing, are not talked about and are kept out of the public eye as much as possible. Occasionally an article will appear in the national press, but it quickly disappears from our consciousness. In 2006, the University of Limerick commissioned a study that found many jockeys in Ireland were dangerously close to life-threatening illness, including chronic dehydration, lack of bone density, inadequate body fat and rotten teeth, due to 'flipping', or vomiting up food just eaten. It is true that riding weights have been raised, but only by a very small amount. The vital and mind-boggling statistic is that the average body weight of trainees entering the industry in Ireland has increased by 37 per cent since 1979 and riding weights by only 6 per cent. Some jockeys, most notably Frankie Dettori, have argued vociferously and passionately for an increase in the weight allowance but there are others, the naturally smaller men, who want it to stay exactly as it is because this means that they get more rides. Dettori maybe a champion but with a riding weight of little more than 8 stone he is a champion who cannot ride a lot of horses for which the handicap dictates a lower weight.

Quite apart from the health risks, there are the safety risks, too. Since 1980, in the UK and Ireland twelve jockeys have been killed on the track. The end has often been brutal: crushed or trampled to death with a finality that is very dark indeed. Falls on the flat are far rarer than those over fences but, because of the speed the horses are travelling at on the flat, when a pile-up does occur, death and injury often go hand in hand. In the USA and Australia the record is even worse. Since 1940, when records began, in the US 148 jockeys have been killed and in Australia there have been more than 300 deaths since 1847.

The injuries sustained are nearly always horrible, mostly to the head, brain and the spine. The ferocity of the damage brought about by half a ton of racehorse landing on you can really only be imagined. Internal injuries, severed necks, snapped spinal cords, these are all a fact of everyday life for jockeys. But for me, now well into my self-imposed regime, I begin to realize what a totally different life I would have had if I had followed my dreams into the horse world. It is clear that, even though I have been around this world all my life, much of the truth of it has remained obscured until now. I doubt I would have lasted long.

By the end of July, however, I know that I can succeed in my own way. It was while returning from another gallop that I realized I could live without the gluttonous excesses that had defined my life for twenty years, and that I am happier now than I have been for a very long time. The temptation to drink and eat has more or less been eradicated. It is as if I am living in a different world. There are no hunger pangs; the lads in a racing yard just do not eat and although Charlie occasionally goes on huge binges I am not tempted to join him. It's a sort of game for me to see if I can succeed where he has been unable to. As the days and weeks go by and the pounds drop off, I begin to understand what the life of the anorexic is like. I get a huge, inexplicable kick from not eating, or eating very little, as part of a diet that is totally alien to me. There is an iron discipline that does not allow me to sway now. I have not fallen off the wagon as I had done, even a few months ago. I have not spoken about this to anyone, least of all Rose, but, in truth, I don't really miss food at all and, remarkably, I do not miss drinking either.

What I do miss, though, is my family. I ring the children every morning at breakfast time just before they go to school. While they are scoffing bacon and eggs and hot buttered toast I am just getting off another horse and thinking about a cup of coffee. In the afternoons, between mealtimes and the excruciatingly hot baths I continue to take to drain myself of even more excess weight, I retreat to bed to conserve my energy and I lie in the dark with the curtains drawn, thinking about the life in London that I have put to one side. Apart from my family, I don't miss what I now see as the drudgery of that life at all. The children are growing up quickly; although I have only been away for a few months, they have changed very subtly.

The London routine is dull in comparison to my present regime. Rose rises, makes a pot of Earl Grey and returns to bed. We drink our tea then wake the children, go to the kitchen with the newspapers, have breakfast then I shave and shower. I then cycle with Lara to school while Jack catches the bus to go to his school. I am at my desk at around 10 a.m. and, unless there is a deadline to be met, I manage to distract myself with really important things like buying mothballs, ringing John Konig, the wine merchant, tidying my desk or rehanging pictures. Most of it is lovely, regimented stuff – it happens every day and every day I think about riding, racing and whether I could transport the children to that domain. The big, airy house on the top of the Berkshire Downs. I sometimes imagine that we all live there and we are all among horses and that is our life. It is a fantasy, of course, but it is nevertheless an interesting one because, when I think about it, I believe it: I think I could have been that jockey, that trainer in that house with that wife and those children.

Chapter Eleven

The time has come to find a race. I had been to Wincanton racecourse on numerous occasions, and through the summer I had it in mind that this was where I would reach the climax of my adventure. It is a wide-open galloping course with old-fashioned stands and it has a particularly rustic feel about it. Farmers, landed families, grandees and racing buffs spend freezing, windswept afternoons at the almost square-shaped track gambling, drinking and roistering. It is south-west England's premier racetrack where, years before, my maternal grandfather, Percy Hazzard, had dragged along my mother every Boxing Day for the highlight meeting of the year. As a young man Percy had even ridden at Wincanton. I wanted to race there because of my grandfather, because my mother was brought up on a farm down the road with horses that she daren't go near, let alone ride; and because if Slades Farm had skipped a generation my life would have been very different indeed.

Jumping the gun, I had already started to tell friends and family that I would be racing at Wincanton, and already a large number had booked themselves into hotels and restaurants in the West Country to watch the great event. They would almost certainly be disappointed. To be surrounded by people keen on horses, racing and food in the environs of the Castleman Hotel in Chettle was a huge pot of gold at the end of a rather austere rainbow.

The first thing I did was to ring the clerk of the course at Wincanton to ask about entry forms for a race that I had in my diary. I had found a race on 26 October (September races being thin on the ground and my weight not being the requisite). A race had been pencilled in for months, but there were three to choose from. It was a date with destiny. Or, rather, it wasn't. Steven Clarke, the managing director of Wincanton, told me that they had cancelled the race this year as it wasn't as popular as it should have been last year.

I had known about the race for years since it was a well-attended annual fixture. In previous year it had attracted some high-profile entries, including Lester Piggott and the Queen's granddaughter, Zara Phillips. With all the goodwill in the world it had still fallen victim to two of the most prevalent problems in the racing industry – a lack of staying power and a dearth of imagination. While other sports have marketed themselves brilliantly, racing is still perceived to be run by an army of clueless retirees, as a gentlemen's club with little regard for the punter. An amateur race with a fat bloke who has lost nearly four stone to fulfil a childhood dream of lining up to run a horse race would be manna from heaven for any other sport, but not, it would seem, to Wincanton racecourse. Since the golden days of the 1970s, the racing industry has fallen on hard times, with fewer and fewer broadcasters lining up to secure television or radio rights. So desperate has the situation become in the attempt to attract terrestrial broadcasters that the sport has resorted to paying them to televise races rather than the other way round.

Within five minutes of digesting the news that the race was off, blind panic set in. I rang Sarah Oliver, who runs the Amateur Jockeys Association (AJA). Without people like Sarah there might not be a racing industry in Great Britain at all. Home Counties and as keen as mustard on all things equine, she should have been my first port of call. Sarah had no idea that the race had been abandoned but told me not to worry because there was another race for which I would be eligible, at Chepstow, a big galloping course just over the England–Wales border.

She told me that the race would be restricted to twelve horses and riders. But, because they had some appalling, unfit jockeys in the past, who had been unable to ride, she would need a cast-iron undertaking from my trainer that I was up to the job. I asked her what previous jockeys had been like; why was she being so cautious about the entry level? 'They were really bad,' she said. 'And were there any accidents?' She was gloomily silent on the point so I didn't press it. To make me feel even better, she said I would need to get £1,000 in sponsorship money. My first thought was 'no bad thing' since it would take my mind off other things like falling off and being run away with. I was sure that I could raise the money but what she said next left me speechless. 'The money raised is for a spinal injuries charity.' I felt like saying, 'What the fuck do you mean? Why not raise it for the Idiot Injured Amateur Jockey Fund', that way the money would go round in a circle and come straight back to me. I asked Sarah if she got the irony and after a few oohs and ahhs she said she did, adding, as an afterthought, that she thought I was 'terribly brave!'.

The Spinal Injuries Association's motto is 'because life needn't stop when you're paralysed'. This was not really what I wanted either to know or hear. The sport has its very own charity, the Injured Jockeys Fund. How many other sports can boast this, I wondered out loud. My heart began to pound, and for the first time I doubted the intelligence of having set out on this venture at all.

A race at Chepstow, a course I have never even visited, would be a very different matter from a race at Wincanton. Still, Chepstow beckoned so I had to deal with Chepstow. Charlie didn't think it was such a bad idea anyway. 'Chepstow is one of the few courses where I've never had a winner,' he says, giving me a knowing look. The set-up of the race aside, preparations are coming along nicely. I am up with the dawn chorus, and down in the yard, even before Trigger now. I take my saddle from its stand and the bridle from its hook, march across the yard to where Pony is, tack him up then wait for the long hollah from Albert. 'Come along, jockeys,' he bellows. We all bring our horses out of their boxes. There is a flurry of activity, riders being legged up, others circling, waiting for the moment they will be hoisted into the saddle and onto the back of whatever horse they are riding. Then off to the gallops. We are all supposed to have read the board before-hand, which tells us who is riding what and the amount of exercise they are doing and at what pace. Early on I learnt to memorize this carefully, otherwise there would be trouble from Trigger. Pony is used as a 'lead' horse up the gallops for some of the younger, more difficult ones. This means that I need to restrict his pace so that the younger, flightier horses behind settle into their own rhythm as they follow his example.

When we get back to the yard I take Pony's saddle off and queue up to give him a cold shower, washing off the pints of sweat and the mud on his legs and his belly, as I do every morning. I am not at all sure that I have performed sufficiently well enough for Trigger to let me ride a proper race-horse yet, even though I am itching for him to give me the word.

Having ridden out twice, I return to the house, exhausted. But after a cigarette and a cup of coffee to restore some energy, I change into tracksuit and trainers and run down the gravel drive, out onto the lane and off down into a dip, then a rising piece of road for a mile. Next to me in a field on the right is the long retired Mely Moss, a horse that won nearly £200,000 in prize money and was one of Charlie's most brilliant training feats when very nearly landing the 2000 Grand National for him. He went off at 25-1 and after four miles of sweat and mud and grief and brutality was beaten by just over a length. Although Charlie never reads the reports on his own races, the newspapers all agreed that it was a brilliant piece of training.

After half a mile I begin to sweat properly again, and the T-shirt I started in at the crack of dawn starts to warm up again. Warm sweat seeps from the pores in the small of my back. The energy drains from my legs but all the while, knowing that I have to do this to get from A to B on my wider journey, I am loving it. I have never enjoyed the pain so much. I inhale a double gulp of air and just keep at it, doing everything I can to stop myself from slowing to a walk. After half an hour I am completely spent but thoroughly invigorated.

On reaching the back door of the house I go in and make another cup of strong, black coffee, smoke a cigarette and retreat to my room where I strip in front of the mirror and look at myself. There is still a long way to go. I take my day clothes into the bathroom and run a bath, once again as hot as I can bear to get into. Gently, tentatively, I lower myself into the steaming water and lie there perspiring until I cannot tell what is water and what is sweat. Five minutes later I run more hot water. I am really boiling up now. Staggering out of the bath, I lie on the floor, glassy, silvery stars swirling around me, thinking that I might pass out. Five minutes elapse and I get up and take in deep breathes of country air, feeling my lungs expanding as I do.

As part of my routine, in the afternoon if Charlie is around I follow him while he inspects his horses, tottering from box to box with a large stick in his hand, helping the lads feed the inmates. One afternoon we all assemble in the tack room and Charlie comes in to mark up the board for the following morning's riding regime. Instead of my riding 2 x Pony I find I am riding 1 x Pony and 1 x Cote Soleil. This is the most significant development so far in my time at Heads Farm as it appears that I have made the grade. Charlie goes off to his office, to indicate that it is business as usual, and I return to the house to get some rest. In truth, I am so excited that I can hardly sit still, and by the time Charlie arrives back at the house for dinner I have not slept a wink. To celebrate I cook us both dinner.

There's a parrot at Heads Farm called Humphrey, who lives in the kitchen. His vocabulary is not only wide-ranging but he never shuts up. Every time I stand in the kitchen, concentrating on putting lunch or dinner together, Humphrey is in the background carrying on his monologue. He can imitate the noise of water running down the plughole in the sink, and if you get too close he'll say, 'Come on give us a kiss', or ask how you are this evening. In a very high-pitched squeal he often catches me by surprise: 'Dommmmminnnnic.' And then he blows a series of raspberries and one big kiss. He is part of the colour and excitement that make up Heads Farm, and the only orders I have heard being barked at Charlie or Trigger have come from him.

Charlie is clueless about cooking. It is said that he can't boil an egg and, if Mr McGregor his gardener is to be believed, can't even open a can of beans. For the duration of my stay at Heads Farm I become the cook as well, and that night we have grouse with pearl barley, a meal that would probably be top of the list for my last supper. First I finely chop half an onion, one clove of garlic, one carrot and a stick of celery, gently fry all this in two tablespoons of olive oil on a low heat for five minutes, turning occasionally. Into the mix I add two generous handfuls of pearl barley and stir in for 1–2 minutes, before adding a pint of chicken stock and simmering for 20–25 minutes, adding more stock as the barley dries out. This I then season with salt and pepper and serve with two young grouse, with olive oil and salt and pepper rubbed in, which I cook on a baking tray on the top shelf of a very hot oven for 20–25 minutes. This is washed down with black coffee with a slug or two of Pusser's rum. Charlie is delighted, and he can see that I am chomping at the bit to get out and ride Cote Soleil. 'I think you're ready. I didn't think you'd do it, to be honest, but you've impressed Trigger, so it's time to ride a proper racehorse.' I struggle to hide my pride, and busy myself by gathering up the grouse carcases to make a deliciously gamey stock to be used in further bean and grain dishes. We watch the BBC ten o'clock news and I go to bed knowing that in the morning I will ride a real racehorse.

Racehorses are as different from other horses as it is possible to be. They are taken out of their natural herd environment in which they spend days grazing and wandering. They sleep very little, maybe in twenty-minute snatches, and seldom lie down. The fear of the predator is foremost. Horses are made to jump and are spooked by a whole variety of seemingly harmless objects or occurrences. A pile of leaves, a black dustbin bag or a high wind will all spook horses and have them running into the line of an oncoming lorry, a barbed wire fence or depositing the jockey on the floor. The injuries to both horse and rider can be, and often are, horrendous.

In their natural environment horses live on a high-fibre, low-protein diet. The small stomach of the horse is nearly always full. The aim of the racehorse trainer and the jockey is to get the horse to run as fast as possible over a given distance. In order that they don't injure themselves they are stabled, covered with rugs, have their coats clipped off to stop them sweating and are fed high-energy food.

Most racehorses are potty. They are bred that way and kept that way in order that they can gallop flat out at speeds approaching 50 mph, with a jockey on top and no more than a small pad of leather for a saddle. The only control the rider has over them is a pair of reins for what limited steering and braking is possible. This is a very different proposition from the cowboy saddles that resemble armchairs and the severe, pivoted bits that will stop a Quarter Horse or Saddlebred in its tracks. The idea is to get the racehorse to move forward continually, not to buck, rear or charge off but to move forward with purpose and pace, to barge, to clip the heels of the horse in front and stretch the neck out as the winning post approaches. As I was about to find out, it doesn't always work out that way.

After my first ride that morning I put Pony back in his box and walk next door to tack up Cote Soleil with his saddle and bridle. Cote Soleil is covered in three large rugs which I undo and slip off him, suffering his opprobrium and distaste as he flattens his ears on his neck and walks around his box snarling at me like a bad-tempered dog. Strangely, I feel no fear, just a pleasure, a warmth and a confidence that I have never felt before in the presence of a horse making ugly faces and threatening to kick my head in.

Cote Soleil is a very different kind of beast from Pony. The winner of nearly £40,000, he is perhaps past his prime but is nevertheless a proper racehorse. Chestnut in colour, about sixteen hands high and of much slighter build, he becomes perfectly well mannered as we make our way down across the partridge-specked Berkshire downland to the gallops. I head off with my new Ukrainian friend, Kirill. I ask him what Cote Soleil is like, and whether he will run away with me. Ever so matter of factly, the Ukrainian turns round in the saddle and says: 'You soon find out he a bit strong, ha, ha, ha.' Thanks, Kirill.

Up at the gallops we do the same routine as before, and circle below the track, before taking a quick right-hander, and then whoosh! This is a very different proposition to Pony. At first Cote Soleil's head is at right angles to his body and he is pulling and prancing like a circus pony. I let the reins go a little, just half an inch, and he's off. I pat him and touch him and feel his neck, all the time thinking that at this speed I am about to lose control and he's about to head off to Hungerford. After three gargantuan pulls, he settles, although he gallops at twice the speed of Pony, the fastest I've ever been, As we get to the top of the hill I realize it has taken forty-five seconds to travel half a mile. I can feel under the huge Alexandra work-wear thermal jacket, which I purchased in a Wantage charity shop for a fiver the day before, that I am dripping with sweat. My back aches and I am puffing as hard as he is. I am ecstatic. That was a real gallop on a real racehorse. It is everything I hoped it would be.

Chapter Twelve

Even though, until this adventure began, I had not ridden a horse for twenty years, horses have been a constant theme in my life. In the afternoons at Heads Farm as I wandered around the stables it was not difficult for me to understand why I had been drawn to these animals in the first place. While it is true that girls and ponies go hand in hand, at around the age of fourteen they discover boys and the ponies are put to one side. With boys it tends to be different; the pull is more enduring, the passion more intense, and, once they have caught the horsing bug, it usually sticks.

One school of thought has it that the draw to be around horses may be caused by a genetic disposition. The big racing communities of Newmarket and Lambourn appear to intermarry at a prodigious rate. But environmental influences are not the only cause cited for our impulse to be surrounded by horses. There is another, more scientific, theory.

Horses are often used therapeutically with emotionally and mentally ill and handicapped children and adults. In February 2009, for example, the emotionally challenged ex-footballer Paul Gascoigne underwent a pioneering treatment called Equine Assisted Psychotherapy (EAP), involving interaction with horses, and pronounced himself cured of his demons. In one exercise Gazza was blindfolded and told to put a saddle on a horse. He asked no one for help, approached the horse from the wrong end and it kicked him – 'Harder than any defender ever kicked me,' he said. The point that was made to Gazza was that you can't do everything on your own; teamwork must play a part. And then, standing in a bleak, windswept field, a horse approached him. 'I was thinking about this one particular horse, and then it came over and started nudging me, it was just incredible. I know it sounds odd but, believe me, it is very powerful,' said Gazza.

It is a pioneering treatment that is gaining more credence by the day, and in many cases the treatment seems to work. In the USA there are entire farms devoted to treating children, adolescents and troubled grown-ups through EAP. Unfortunately, Gazza was not going to help the cause. In February 2010, a year after his initial treatment, he was arrested for drunk-driving.

Nevertheless, I was fascinated by this. Research carried out by Julie K. Trevelyan, an equine coordinator at a ranch in Aspen, Colorado, specialising in EAP, backed it up when she spoke of how many of her students arrived without a horse background and took to the treatment immediately.

The treatment involves very little mounted work. Rather the patient is encouraged to form a relationship with the horse, to communicate with it and to take responsibility for the animal in its care. The treatment is used mainly on children and adults who have been through mainstream psychotherapy without any discernible relief.

According to Trevelyan, EAP essentially reveals insights through analogy and metaphor. By relating their experiences with the horses to other people and issues in their lives, the students can begin to examine their negative behaviour and understand how to change them into positive behaviour. Another benefit of EAP is that the activities inherently demand an immediate reaction from the students. As I know to be confronted with a horse for the first time can be a very frightening experience, full of stress but if you can learn to harness the fear and build a relationship with the horse it can become a very powerful tool indeed. The treatment has a good success rate and is becoming a more accepted and mainstream science in the US. It has also started in a small way in the UK. It also happens that one of the most common conditions it is used to treat is Attention-Deficit Hyperactivity Disorder (ADHD). ADHD is a condition that affects many young adults, predominantly boys. It leaves sufferers with little ability to concentrate, and they constantly flit between distractions, unable to keep their attention on one thing for very long. As well as being very disruptive, they have little empathy for those around them. All this sounded very familiar.

The more I read about EAP and the more I learnt about the types of people who submit themselves to it, the more I realized that was my story, too. It explained why, as a child, it had only been when I was around horses that I was able to remain calm for long stretches at a time, why I had made life for my parents so difficult. My mother, the psychologist, never spotted it, but looking out of the bedroom window at the lads mucking out the stables, calmer, happier, more at peace than I had been for as long as I could remember, I wondered whether all of us here were, inadvertently, putting ourselves through a process of self-medication.

*   *   *

By the middle of September I have been living on and off at Heads Farm for six months. That afternoon I get a message from the HSBC saying that we are in danger of breaching our overdraft limit. We are considerably overdrawn and have been battening down the hatches for the economic downturn. We also receive an unexpectedly huge bill for school fees. On the drive back to London I reflect on the cost of my taking so long off, and, sitting in traffic surrounded by a week of horse riding kit and old clothes, whether I have gone a bit potty. Even for the richest people involved in horses it is an expensive hobby, and what Sheikh Mohammed and I at least have in common is that we are both living proof that nothing sensible has ever happened when you put horses and money together.

On my return I went to see the Portuguese butcher across the street from us. He looked very sheepish, and refused to look me in the eye. I asked him what the matter was. 'Are you OK?' he said. 'What do you mean?' I replied. 'You look terrible, you have lost so much weight. You must be ill.' I then told him about my dream and he laughed and said, 'Good for you, I am glad you are not ill.' Although this was not the first time someone had commented on my rapidly vanishing girth, it was encouraging to hear that the change looked so dramatic.

Desperate for more exercise, I go off and play tennis with Ralph on the Royal Hospital courts in Chelsea. My physical weakness is underlined by my losing six-love whereas earlier in the summer I had won six-two. While out with the horses the adrenalin is enough to keep me going for the whole morning; on the tennis court I can hardly move for fatigue.

Ralph notices that my serve is feeble and asks if anything is wrong. This is the first time I have felt so exhausted and it's a sign that the combination of the diet and exercise are catching up on me. I think I may have pushed it too far this time, since all I have eaten is a tiny breakfast bowl of porridge and barley. But, as I explain to Ralph, this is what jockeys are faced with on a daily basis, and I am one of them now. Cycling home, Ralph still looks worried and tells me that I need to eat something and get some rest. I nod obediently, but the moment I get through the door I run the hottest bath the boiler can give me and sink into the water, wishing away the pounds. Half an hour later I climb out and, exhausted, collapse into bed and sleep for two hours before I pick at my lunch – a tiny salad and a small bowl of lentils – my appetite for a rich, wholesome meal washed down with a bottle of red now ancient history.

While I have now almost completely stopped drinking, Rose is keen not to let my routine spoil her own habits, and I feel rather sanctimonious about not joining her for a glass. Even though it is the first time in a long while that we have been at home together on our own, I know now that I have more or less nailed the diet and that it is simply a matter of carrying on doggedly for just two more months. When she tries to serve me an extra helping of dinner I decline, quietly at first, before having to refuse the advance of the laden spoon more forcefully. I do not say it, and neither does Rose, but we can both tell that something is wrong. It is no longer the weight, since I have found a new agility and spring onto a horse when Albert legs me up in the morning. And I am finally now riding out on Cote Soleil every day, so there is no excuse for impatience on that front.

It is only when I am back in London that I become irritable around the house and it takes me a while to realize what the problem is. This London life doesn't feel quite right, even though it is an ordinary Sunday evening with my family. I consider what excuse I can give to the children and pack my bags. My home is Heads Farm now, and it is the only place I feel comfortable. The next time I see the children will be when they come to watch me ride at the farm.

As soon as I am in the car heading back to Heads Farm, though, I am racked with guilt about having created such a distance between myself and my former life, and, of course, especially the family. I am not entirely sure when this happened to me, but it is clear that this adventure is starting to become something of an obsession. Until recently, no matter how much I enjoyed being at Heads Farm, home was always home. Now, though, I can visualize the race, and we have started to talk more seriously about the preparations I need to undertake in the final weeks. I know now everything I need to know about the jockey's life, from how to put the saddle and bridle on, the timing of getting to the gallops, to how to handle the different horses and spot their moods. Most importantly, perhaps, I know how Charlie and Trigger and all the lads will react in particular situations. I have finally become one of them.

Once I arrive back at Heads Farm and I have unpacked, Charlie suggests that, instead of me cooking dinner, we retire to the Ibex Inn for the evening where a delicious beef stew is served. It's also good for my self-discipline to be around beer and wine and spirits and basketsful of warm bread and mountainous slices of cheese.

On the way Charlie again talks about his diet and warns me not to let him eat bread or cheese. I have a few runner beans as an accompaniment. Charlie orders a bowl of peas and carrots, two pints of water, a packet of digestive biscuits and an entire plateful of Yarg, a creamy Cornish cheese that he has a passion for, consisting of four normal portions. At least this time he manages to keep clear of the bread.

At the Ibex we meet Barry and Janet Marsden. Originally from Birmingham, they now live in Devon and run a couple of grain and wholefoods stores, the profits of which they recycle by buying more grain and wholefoods for racehorses, some of which are trained by Charlie. For couples like Barry and Janet, for whom horses are a passion and a hobby, business and sentimentality don't mix well. When they buy a horse, no matter how bad it is they keep it for life. While Charlie teases them about shooting the useless ones that he trains for them, Janet tells me about a breeding programme they have just embarked upon. Having spent thousands on a nomination – the right to send a nominated mare to mate with a stallion – they have now embarked on a full-scale, albeit tiny, breeding programme. They say they'll sell the progeny but I know that they'll just get Derby fever and hang onto it and send it to Charlie to be trained.

There are tens of thousands of people like Barry and Janet in the UK and there are hundreds of trainers chasing after them. They are lucky they've got Charlie. If you explained to Charlie how to crook someone he just wouldn't understand why people do it. He has witnessed all manner of people steal money from naïve, stupid and ill-informed owners but such is his honesty and love for his sport that he doesn't want to see potential owners and good people put off by the rogues and vagabonds who hang around the industry.

While owners like Barry and Janet, and trainers like Charlie, get very emotional about their horses, the horses themselves can be aggressive and timid, frightened and stubborn, but they rarely reciprocate your emotions. They have very little real passion, shed no tears, show no gratitude and have little time for forgiveness. We delude ourselves into thinking that they care about us at all and we are prone to misinterpreting their behaviour. That whinny over the stable door is not for you or me; it is for the food we are about to give them. They are brutal and bullying and uncaring and selfish. And yet, here we are, four adults talking about them as if they were our own children, and I wonder why we love them and why my new friends from Birmingham love them, too.

The reason, I think, is that we like to believe that they are there for us and will do as we ask them, since they were our first servants. They run faster and jump higher because they can and perhaps because they want to, not to please us, but to please themselves. In return for their time, energy and effort we might reward them with a few pats, a bowl of oats and a few handfuls of hay. Crucially, horses are not judgemental and I think that is why, all those years ago, I was first attracted to them. On the way back in the car Charlie tells me that the Marsdens have a good horse called The Local that he thinks they might let me ride in the race. The Local is not at the yard so will have to be brought back into training. He's had a lay-off but Charlie says he should be relatively fit.

The next day my two lots are much later than usual and I get to the yard at 8 a.m. for the second and third outings. I am still riding out on Pony every morning to work on my technique, and on the Home gallops I am getting him going as fast as he has ever gone for two five-furlong spurts before taking him back to the yard and onto Cote Soleil for a Home gallops canter. I no longer feel like a complete amateur when I get on and off; I don't feel that the lads are laughing as heartily as they used to about the fat bloke from London. They tell me I look slimmer and fitter and there are little nuances when a horse jibs or jolts, where previously they would have been worried about what I was doing to the horse. As we ride up the gallops together, I can now stay in touch with the best of them. Some are even starting to ask about my race date, and I even heard two of them say that they thought I was actually quite a good jockey.

After we have been up Home gallops, the rest of the lads return to the yard. Meanwhile, Peter, a Czech who speaks very bad English, and I set off for Summerdown gallops, a big, rangy all-weather track about two miles from Heads Farm. We hack through a corn field that is being cut and memories of thirty years ago return to haunt me. I touch Cote Soleil on the neck, he shakes his head and I realize there is nothing to worry about and that I am less nervous than I have ever been. Charlie is in two minds about racing him, though. He says that, at the age of eleven, he is too slow to have a real chance but he is undoubtedly a good schoolmaster, and he still has lots to teach me. Even after two months of riding him, I find that Cote Soleil is still boisterous and sometimes bad-tempered in the stable, but he is gradually giving me back my confidence. With confidence comes better riding. I have a lighter touch on the reins, am stronger in the legs. I don't jump when he jumps; I just feel his neck and talk to him in a low, gentle voice.

We hack through the undergrowth for several miles. Pheasants jump out of the hedgerow; the sun fights to come out, while the breeze is cool. We trot along a westerly road and through a farmyard and, as we turn the bend, I see Peter pull up his stirrups into the knees-under-nostrils position. I do the same and as we round the corner there is an all-weather gallop marked out. I can only see the beginning since it's on a steep hill, and I don't know how long we are going for, although I had anticipated that it must be longer than five furlongs otherwise we would have stayed on the Home gallop. Peter and his horse jump off in unison. Peter's mount, eager and fiery and ready to get on with the job, lifts his forelegs off the ground. He crouches onto his hind legs and flies like a stone from a tautly pulled catapult up the gallop. Cote Soleil sees what is happening and wants to get on with it. I shorten up the reins and pivot my weight forward against him. My stirrup leathers are short, the accelerator is flat against the floor and we take off. This moment is what eight months of training has been all about.

Back he goes onto his hind legs and, whoosh, we're off. It's only as we round the first bend that I realize this is something of an undertaking. The one-furlong post shoots up to my right, I try to steady him but he's anxious to keep up with and then overtake Peter's horse. Two, three, four furlongs – the white posts marking them out to my right fly by and then as we hit the five-furlong post Cote Soleil settles and does something extraordinary. He takes in a huge lungful of air. While at full tilt, his flanks expand and push my legs out away from his side as he swallows the stuff that will keep him going, the air that will stop him falling under me and expiring; another furlong and another gulp of air.

In all the years of riding horses I have never experienced the brutality of the horse gasping for air, and his ability to time it so perfectly is a wonder. He is loving it. As we pass the halfway mark I see from the corner of my eye Trigger sitting in Charlie's car by the trackside, assessing my every move. This is the first proper gallop I have had and Trigger is watching over me, or that's what I like to think. In all likelihood he is watching over Cote Soleil, making sure I don't run him into a tree and kill him. As we finish Trigger doesn't say anything but I know he'll give Charlie a gallops report and tell him how I've done. On the way back he passes us in the lane and I get a nod of recognition, nothing more. For the rest of the day I worry that I've made a huge mess of what should have been my two minutes of glory, the point where I should have thought to myself, 'I'm on the way, I'm in one piece.' From now on anything is possible.

On the way back to Heads Farm I hope that Peter will say something to indicate that he thought I had done well. He doesn't say anything either but does allow me to bum a fag off him. I try to get a conversation going to encourage him to tell me what he thinks of my riding. All he volunteers is that he will shortly be returning to the Czech Republic. He says he wants to follow his father into the police force but I know that he'll get back and he won't be able to let go of this world for too long. He is such a nice rider and has a real empathy with the horse and we will all be sad to see him go.

Having ridden my two lots, I go back to the house, change, go for a run and take my ritual hot bath. I then drive to Wantage to visit the Boots the chemist. I stand on the scales, put in the money and press a button. The machine prints a ticket which it discreetly pops out – face down. I keep it face down and wait until I get back to Heads Farm before retrieving it from my pocket and turning it over on the kitchen table. The suspense kills me every time I do this, but I keep up the routine since it is another form of discipline.

Standing at the kitchen table, I furtively look at the ticket. It reads 12 stone 10lb. No wonder the Portuguese butcher was concerned about my health. That's more than three stone lost. I unpack the fruit and vegetables I bought from one of the market stalls – rocket, cucumber, lettuce, broccoli and cauliflower – and make a very light lunch for Charlie and myself.

Later in the afternoon I wander over to Charlie's office and watch a horse he has in the yard run in a televised race. Dr Livingstone unexpectedly wins a £6,000 handicap at odds of 33-1. I venture to think that if I had wagered £1,000 the overdraft would, very nearly, be a thing of the past. If I had and it had lost the crisis would have deepened somewhat but the risk:reward ratio surely would have been worth it. I kick myself. Albert gives me the depressing news that none of the lads were on the horse either, not even with an each-way bet. We retire back to the house and I cook some pearl barley in stock and roast another brace of grouse. Earthy, bloody and with a wonderful nutty flavour.

The following morning the first lot pulls out just after seven. I have not slept well, and am not concentrating as I get Cote Soleil ready. Trigger notices that my saddle is not straight, and that all the pads are too far back and in danger of slipping. I smile at him, not impolitely, just to break the ice and admit my stupidity, but he misconstrues the gesture. 'You won't be bloody well laughing when that lot slips back as you're doing forty miles an hour up the gallops.' I've seen it for myself on a racecourse before: if the saddle slips it can spell disaster. The result that time was that the terrified horse hurtled off through the rails, narrowly avoiding children and pensioners. I get off smartly and move the saddle forward.

Bianca is riding a two-year-old filly called Sister Clement. On the way back from the gallops we chat about what she wants to do with her life. 'Marry rich man. You find me one, perhaps?' she asks. She says how much she loves Pony, who she rides when I am not here. At this point, and for no apparent reason, Sister Clement turns nasty and lets fly with both back hooves. The reach and power of the filly is frightening and I feel the breeze as her hoofs pass my face. No one had seen it coming and I was completely shocked. I contemplated what would have happened if she had kicked me in the face. If her hoofs had hit the target I would have been dead. Dead like Tony Bennett, the man my mother and her sisters sold Slades Farm to, who was kicked squarely in the face by a horse and died instantly. Sister Clement was intending to kick Pony, not me, but even so the episode underlines just how careful you have to be around these highly strung animals. Bianca looks shocked, too, but holds on boldly and doesn't get deposited. But Sister Clement and her hind legs keep turning over in my mind. I had almost planned my funeral. Who would turn up? What would they say? It is at times like this that you get a sense of your own mortality. What the cigarettes haven't yet done, Sister Clement nearly did in a split second. It's the equine equivalent of being knocked over and killed by a bus. I make sure that I give Sister Clement a very wide berth from now on.

The following week I go to Wantage on my usual trip to the fruit and veg and fish stalls and, of course, to weigh myself at Boots. I have lost five pounds in one week. I now weigh 12 stone 5lb. I nearly go off and have a drink to celebrate.

Charlie, I have now realized, falls prey to all sorts of voodoo practitioners. In all the time I have been staying with him, trying to get him to eat as I eat, he has barely lost any weight at all. What he doesn't admit (but is clear to me now) is that he is looking for a quick fix for his weight problem that will allow him to carry on eating and drinking exactly as he wishes. Various Indian, Chinese and other assorted mystics in London are more than willing to take his coins and sing the tune he wants to hear. He is still enormous but he has found an acupuncturist who goes some way to convincing him that he can continue to eat pretty much what he likes as long as he has a host of needles stuck into his backside at regular intervals. Even when he does eat well he eats so much stuff that he'd be better off having a loaf of bread or a plate of chips. If you eat twenty lettuces, a dozen oat bars and thirty cucumbers of course you are going to put on weight but Charlie doesn't get the basic principle that if you eat less you'll lose weight.

Later that day, and quite unbelievably, the Chepstow race falls apart, too. Sarah Oliver rings me and says that, due to an administrative error, Chepstow is not going to happen. She suggests various other venues, including Bangor-on-Dee. It is the end of September, and I am supposed to be less than a month away from my big day. I am momentarily left speechless. Bangor-on-Dee is not my idea of fun, and I politely decline. Then I have a brainwave.

Poring over the racing calendar, desperately seeking a race meeting that might be able to fit me and eleven other jockeys and horses into the schedule, I see that in the first week of November there's a meeting at Towcester, a track in Northamptonshire that any trainer will tell you is one of the most challenging and rewarding courses in the country. Jumping off from the start, there's a big downhill camber where a horse can easily become unbalanced, a tight right-hand bend and then a straight along the bottom of the track before a huge hill to climb before arriving up in front of the stands and the winning post. The hill catches out all sorts of good horses, and the very stiff finish makes the famous hill at Cheltenham look like the finish of a donkey derby.

Chris Palmer runs the finances and investments for the Hesketh family and he has been to shoot with us at Chettle.

The Hesketh family also just happen to own Towcester race-course and there is a scheduled race meeting on 6 November. Palmer is a very unfussy, down-to-earth type of bloke, so I ring him and ask if there's any possibility of squeezing in another race. A flat race of a mile and a half for amateur jockeys. 'There is and we can,' he says. I ring Sarah Oliver and tell her. She is ecstatic, I am ecstatic, we are all very happy.

With a race date now firmly set, and a guarantee that it will not fall through, I have to get myself ready to lose the final stone, which will be the hardest. I decide really to go for it. With my breakfast of grains, oats, linseed, wheat germ, barley and currants soaked overnight I wash down a handful of laxatives with a cup of Earl Grey as the sun rises. Lunch is a small salad; dinner a bowl of pearl barley and maybe a piece of game or fish with green tea and more laxatives; and then the second of two steaming hot baths of the day. All the lads, being somewhat lighter than me, have little comprehension of what I am going through. They have sympathy, they laugh at me and we have nice times talking about horses they have loved and loathed. I particularly like Josef, who has an understanding and a commitment to the horse and a simple appreciation of what I am trying to achieve. In his broken English he offers words of encouragement and wisdom.

On top of the running and the cigarettes, I also start to go swimming at the local baths in Wantage. The pool is the perfect length for putting in an hour of front crawl, which really tests my stamina, and afterwards I walk up a flight of stairs to the first floor, where there is a very well used sauna. All the lads from Lambourn and the surrounding racing stables with any dream of riding in a race come here to sweat off the excess pounds. They are even given a discount.

The following day, after riding Cote Soleil's first lot and completing two gallops, we return to Heads Farm where an old creaking horsebox arrives to take us the fifteen miles to Compton Down so that I can practise on a proper track. It is a beautiful piling of historic downland with a covering of turf so perfect and so ancient that John tells me it is as near to a perfect preparation as I am going to get. John and I travel with the horses in the lorry while Trigger sits next to the driver, puffing on a big fat cigar. I know that the two of them are worried, if disproportionately, both for me and the horse: that is, 5 per cent for me and 95 per cent for the horse. I ask John what we are about to do and he says: 'Oh, it's just beautiful up there, you wait till you get there, it's the best gallop in the world.' Telling me nothing whatsoever about how short to ride, whether we are going to canter or gallop or how far we are going to run for. We unload the horses onto a vast expanse of plain with the cooling towers of Didcot Power Station, looking like huge hollow elephant's legs, belching out smoke on the horizon. The lorry driver legs us all up and Trigger gives the instructions. Away from the yard Trigger is more relaxed about me. He says that we will trot for a while and then have a slow canter, before we shorten our stirrups as we hit the turf that is marked out with red and white furlong pegs stuck in the ground. Trigger says that as we hit the mile mark I'm to ask Cote Soleil to quicken. He wants me to really go for it as if I'm in a race, that I am to imagine myself chasing down the horses in the final furlong of the Derby. Mounted and ready to go, Cote Soleil trots away enthusiastically and then, as we break into a canter, I am in perfect control. Beneath me he feels fantastic, as though he has understood the instructions perfectly as well.

With Trigger and Charlie behind us, waiting in the car, there is a moment up there on Compton Down when everything suddenly clicks. I struggle to keep the smile off my face as I realize that, at forty-seven, I am actually doing this. It is a poignant moment, and one I can't wait to share with the family when I get home. If my father could have seen me now, he would have been proud. I stroke Cote Soleil's chestnut neck and rub it so the waxy scurf with its smell of chestnuts and soap and lanolin come off him and build up a deposit in my fingertips, just as with Conker all those years ago. And then we are off.

Even a month ago he would have run off with me, but now he trusts me and he settles down into a gallop. Furlong after furlong he really pelts along but I feel safe and comfortable as he huffs and puffs below me. There is huge power beneath me as we tear right and right again. I feel at one with him; everything is going to plan. He is moving along so smoothly that all I have to do is sit still on top of him and let him do the work. He snorts and puffs, the sweat dripping from him, and then we get to the mile marker and I gather him up and lean forward and start to talk words of encouragement at him and … and … he dies on me. He has no more to give. He has tried his heart out for me but there is nothing left. In the last two furlongs, when we should be roaring towards the finishing line, he is knackered, showing every one of his eleven years. But I am safe, in one piece and gloriously happy. There is no judgement about my performance, no post-mortem. I've done it and we're going to Towcester. We're going to race.

Two days later, Cote Soleil goes very badly lame. I didn't ride him the day after the work ride on Compton Down as considered stable wisdom had it that he would be too exhausted, but when I do ride him next we go down to the gallops, turn the corner onto the cinder track and it is only then I realize that he is staggering. I jump off him, pick out his foot but don't find the nail that he has stood on until later in the afternoon. It's a rusty old thing that has lodged itself between shoe and hoof. Albert pulls it out and poultices the foot. Cote Soleil is off for five days and looking very sorry for himself. His head is down when I visit him in the box, as if to say, 'This is all your fault' – and he may not be wrong.

Although I acquitted myself well enough on Compton Down, Cote Soleil is quite clearly not going to be the horse I ride at Towcester. Apart from being lame at the moment, as lovely as he is he is just not quick enough. Charlie's plan to get The Local back into training has backfired somewhat in that the Marsdens say he's having a lovely time in semi-retirement. They do want to get him back into training but not this season. Having found the race, I am now without a horse and mentally begin a downward spiral. Thinking all the time that this is a great adventure, my time at Heads Farm has been one of the most fantastic, exhilarating periods in my life and even if I don't get to Towcester I have done everything in my power to try and get there.

By mid-October, with less than three weeks until my race, Cote Soleil was still off sick and there was a bit of a row in the yard about the nail that had gone through his foot. No one had told Charlie about it, although they had told me. Thinking I was doing the right thing, I mentioned it to Charlie and he exploded at Trigger for not telling him. Later in the day Albert sneered at me: 'I told you not to tell the boss, and you fucking did.' It was my first real mistake while I was there. A very clear line had been drawn. While I thought I was one of the lads, they clearly thought otherwise. I was a friend of the guv'nor and could never really be one of them. Some of the lads thought that I'd been to school with Charlie: 'We all assumed you were an Old Etonian,' one said. As in every facet of racing, no one tells the whole truth. There are lots of assumptions but few hard facts.

*   *   *

While Cote Soleil is laid up I am given a new horse to ride. Dancing Marabout, a slip of a thing, is a three-year-old chestnut gelding sired by Danehill Dancer, a stallion owned by John Magnier. Danehill Dancer's fee for the 2004 covering season was €45,000. Production costs were around the same over the two-year period. Dancing Marabout was sold for 70,000 guineas, so not a lot of profit there for the breeder but a great deal for Mr Magnier. In fact, I would think there was about €4.5 million in it for him if Danehill Dancer had covered a hundred mares that year. But the horse went on to be very successful as a sire and now stands at a so-called 'private' fee which, at its peak, was said to be around €125,00 each time, meaning around €10–15 million of income from one horse each year if he covers a hundred mares, and he certainly does at least that.

Dancing Marabout has won a single, solitary race but is most famous for having been ridden by Frankie Dettori and two other champion jockeys, Ryan Moore and AP McCoy. He is quite a feisty, fiery young fellow, very like a lot of the ponies I rode when I was young. He's nice going down to the gallops and easy to hold, but anxious. He gives me a good gallop and has a lot of fuel in the tank. I know that if I leant forward and whispered 'go' into his ear he would. Last week he threw Bianca. This week it may well be my turn.

On that still sunny morning we are the only pair doing a gallop and he jibs a bit when I point him for home away from the herd, and he promises to be naughty. He dances and pulls, trying to trot when he should be walking and trying to canter when he should be trotting. He snorts, but otherwise is well behaved, until he breaks into a canter and throws his head up and bashes me in the face. Blood spurts from my cheekbone, but surprisingly there's no pain, just blood that drips down onto my hands, onto the reins and down his neck and shoulder. I get back to the yard and see my reflection in a window-pane. I am absolutely covered in blood. It has dripped down onto my sweat jacket and won't congeal. I wash Dancing Marabout down, and take the cold hose to myself to wash the blood off. Trigger sees me and visibly starts at the state of my face. 'Jeeesus, what happened?' he asks. I tell him that it is nothing, that it looks a lot worse than it is. Trigger tells me to record it all in the accident book, which I have studiously avoided since my first day. I go and pat Marabout and am then told he will be the horse that I will ride at Towcester. I retire to the racing office to fill out the accident book and thank the Lord that mine is only a minor injury.

Once I have patched myself up I drive back to Chettle to meet my daughter and Ralph, who have come down for the first day of the shooting season. Lara is visibly shocked by my bashed-up face. She says, too, that she is missing my presence in London but she also asks incessantly about how I am getting on, what horse I am going to ride, how the diet is going, how long the race is. The questions are overwhelming and I have no answers.

Chettle before shooting is normally the place where I'd have a huge meal and lots to drink, but not tonight. While the assembled crowd tuck into gargantuan portions of freshly sliced meat and home-made pies, I make do with a salad and some water. While out shooting the following day, all the old friends, who I have not seen in months, say how ghastly, thin and drawn I look. I also feel like shit. But even here, in Chettle, the place I love and cherish, I feel unsettled. It is as distant to me as London. I actually want to be back at Heads Farm, back on the Berkshire Downs with Charlie and Trigger and all of the lads.

Following the shoot, Lara returns to London with Ralph and I drive back to Heads Farm. Later that week, Charlie has a colt called Calaloo running at Bath and he asks me if I want to travel with him to the racecourse. I leap at the opportunity and, having ridden my three in the morning, I hang around at the house until Charlie's office rings me and says that he'll collect me at noon. 'So be ready,' they add. He arrives twenty minutes late and as we manoeuvre through the lanes of Berkshire he says that we won't be driving after all, but flying instead.

Manton is the home of Guy Sangster, part owner of Calaloo and son of the late Robert Sangster who was not only the original big-money investor behind Coolmore but also a good friend to me when I was making my Lester Piggott documentary. The last time I was at Manton was ten years ago to record the Channel 4 interview with Robert about Piggott. Fortified by a large swig of gin, he had been incredibly honest and gave a remarkably frank interview about Lester's shenanigans on and off the track. This did not endear him to the racing establishment, of which he was a well-known member. He was attacked in the *Racing Post*, the perception being that he had broken a word of honour.

Charlie doesn't know this but one of my greatest fears in life is flying in helicopters, so when we arrive at Manton to be greeted by a pristine helicopter parked on the lawn I start to feel really sick.

Rob Copplestone is a big man with a red face and a licence to fly helicopters. He looks as if he'd be more at home in a gentlemen's club in St James's and nothing that he says before take-off instils me with confidence. The seat belt will not stretch round Charlie's girth and Rob says that 'really I shouldn't fly you because we can't strap you in', but he does nonetheless.

As we take off, Rob talks on his radio to air traffic control and various RAF bases along the way. Meanwhile, I just sit there, unable to hear anything but definitely feeling that I would rather have both feet placed solidly on terra firma. Ten minutes later and we've landed at Bath racecourse. Rob and I hand over piles of notes at the Tote and then go with Charlie and Guy to the parade ring. Charlie has great hopes for Calaloo in the race, and, as we stand around waiting for our jockey, Steve Drowne, to appear I start to feel part of the set-up.

Five minutes later, Calaloo romps home and five minutes after that I have trousered £100 from a £5 stake on the Tote. After a glass of champagne proffered by Bath racecourse we are back off in the chopper to Manton. Later, on the way back to Heads Farm, I tell Charlie that after the helicopter flight with no cigarettes to hand I am now ready to give up, pack them in. Of course I don't.

Chapter Thirteen

There are now less than three weeks to go until we pack up the horsebox and make our way to Towcester. I am riding every day and I can feel that I am getting better and better. The children have asked if they can come and watch me ride. Having conferred with Charlie, we plan for them to pay a visit at half-term, just before the race. Everyone in the stables seems to have an opinion on Dancing Marabout and how to get the best out of him. Charlie and Trigger tell me that, while he has limited acceleration, he is a great stayer. The lads in the stable tell me to 'keep him handy, up with the first four and clip him one if he slackens'. Trigger, on the other hand, says 'start in front and stay there. Hit him anywhere he has fur, anywhere on his coat but keep him in the front.' By the end of the first gallop I am so confused about what I should and shouldn't be doing that I ignore them all and just let him ride out at his own pace. The most important thing at this stage is that we get to know each other before the race, so neither of us gets spooked at the start line.

Two days after Calaloo wins his race at Bath, I walk past his box. Lying in the gutter outside his stable early in the morning is a lump of meat. I am not sure what it is so I ask one of the lads, only to be told 'they are his bollocks'. They aren't joking. Calaloo stands at the back of his box looking sullen, as well he might. I scoop up his knackers, take them back to the house and put them in the fridge. I have it vaguely in mind that I might eat them. I once ate bull's testicles, with the girlfriend who went with me to Ireland, in a restaurant in Seville following a bullfight, and remembered them as being delicious. We spent the afternoon at the bullfight, which was one of the most shocking, exciting, dramatic and bloodthirsty things I think I have ever done. By tradition a restaurant next to the ring served the testicles of the slain bull. They were rather like lamb's kidneys, only larger, stronger and more pungent in taste and texture. As we left the restaurant I remember we both burst out laughing when she said how Moorish they were.

It is a really rum job for a horse when he's run his heart out for Charlie, valiantly pushing his nose first past the post, only to have his balls cut off forty-eight hours later. Trainers are very keen on castrating all but the very best horses, which are spared since they are to be used for stud purposes. They have a huge list of not entirely plausible reasons why colts should be castrated. They range from the blindingly obvious like 'he's too coltish' or that the horse 'won't concentrate,' to the less plausible 'it will sharpen him up'. None of the above seemed to apply to poor old Calaloo, who had just won a race and returned home bathed in glory. Is there no justice in this world, I wondered, as I looked at him sulking at the back of his box? After I'd put the testicles in the fridge I told Trigger on the phone that I was going to cook them for dinner that evening for Charlie. It was only then that Trigger became a bit windy and said, 'For God's sake don't, before they were cut off the vet injected them with something horrible that could kill you'. I took Calaloo's balls out of the fridge and flung them in the bin.

On the first day of half-term, I drive to Newbury station to pick up the family, and I am surprised that I am actually quite nervous. This is the first time that they have come to watch me ride, and the first time that Jack and Lara have been to visit Heads Farm. For months I have been happily leading a double life in which neither half has overlapped with the other; now it is time for the family to see just what I have been sneaking out of the house for. They are full of questions as they sit in the back of the car, and I start to worry that, while they are watching me, I will forget everything that I have learnt.

Once we get to the farm, Rose takes charge of the food while I show the children around the stables and introduce them to Trigger, the lads and to Dancing Marabout. When we get back, Rose has cooked the most fabulous dinner of roast chicken, potatoes and broccoli. Charlie, as usual, wolfs the lot, and demolishes a bottle of red wine with Rose, while I keep to the water. I stick to a green salad with a bit of lean chicken breast. Jack is in television heaven as he is served his dinner sitting in front of Sky on Charlie's giant TV screen. The children sleep in a room adjacent to ours, and it takes me a long time to get to sleep; it feels odd having them here on my territory, a place that I have created, a life that they know virtually nothing about.

Early the following morning, Rose and Lara go out with Charlie and watch me ride. Jack stays in front of the television. It's a straightforward canter, and I feel pretty much in control on Dancing Marabout as I flick past Charlie's car full of interested onlookers. I feel quite self-conscious, too, and can't help asking myself what I must look like in comparison to the other lads, who are riding out with me. Turning my head to the right I can see my reflection in the windows of the car that is parked trackside. I think I look good, but perhaps not as perfectly poised as I imagined I would be. As the French trainer Pascal Bary said, I am not the right shape for a jockey. When we are done and have returned to the stables I ask Lara what she thought. At just ten years old, she knows how to flatter: 'You looked great, Dad, really great. I love you,' she says, before giving me a big wet kiss.

It takes a while to explain to Lara the routine that I am following, and she looks at me quizzically when I tell her that I will meet her after my run and a steaming hot bath. Dressed, exhausted and sucking on a boiled sweet to give me some energy, we drive down to the tack shop on the Great Shefford road to seek out some boots and breeches that I will need for the race. The vest and silk for my hat will be supplied by Charlie, as I will be racing in his colours.

New boots are horribly expensive and the older ones we find are either ill-fitting or just don't fit, full stop. Then Lara spots a pair of boots at the bottom of a box full of equine junk. When I enquire about their origin, I am told that they have been there for more than two years, but as I unzip them I know these are the boots I am going to ride in. The back of them creases around the heel of my foot but otherwise they fit perfectly, and it is hard to believe that they have been hidden away at the bottom of this huge cardboard carton just waiting to be claimed. They have my name on them. Actually, they have the name of the owner scribbled on a brown parcel tag that ties them together through the loops of the zipper that runs up the back of the calf. At two pounds in weight the boots are quite heavy; they also hardly look used at all and I wonder if they are being sold because of a bereavement. Is it possible that the previous owner had an unlucky fall?

The shop assistant is a bit sheepish about their provenance and when I ask her whether the owner would take less than the £60 they're asking she says, 'Oh yes, I'm sure she will. They *were* her husband's and they've been here for years. I'm sure she'll take £50 but I'd better ring her and check.' There is something vaguely fatalistic about her tone. She knows that the owner wants shot of them at any price. The owner isn't in so I agree to go back the following afternoon and collect the boots once the assistant has spoken to their owner.

The breeches I find are wispy thin, and the label says that they were made in Italy. They are the largest size the shop has, however, and like gossamer, and they pull on quite easily once I get my feet through the elasticated lower legs. I stand in the changing room flexing my thigh muscles and smoothing down the white nylon.

By now I am eating very little and shitting perhaps two or three times a week if I am lucky. It is a fine balance between taking enough on board to keep going but not so much as to put on weight. I reckon I have it down to a fine art and can, with a bit of discipline and effort, lose two pounds a day from now on. To the routine of exercise and dieting have been added vast quantities of cigarettes and cups of coffee, and I am now being plagued by the dizzy spells that jockeys talk of, especially when getting out of the bath. There are times when I have to lie flat on my back in the bathroom for half an hour to regain my composure. But I have hit 11 stone 11lb for the first time and have lost five pounds in the past week alone, mostly put down to the fact that I have reduced the diet even further to pinhead oats (1 tbspn), golden linseed (half tbspn), wheatgerm (half tbspn) and a small handful of sultanas. All this is soaked overnight in water and then eaten before riding in the morning: it gives me the right amount of energy for four hours' medium or hard physical work. Lunch is the real struggle as to lose the final pounds I am down to eating a raw salad, either roots such as carrots, beetroot, red cabbage, broccoli, fennel, celery and cucumber or lettuce, cucumber and rocket. Both with an olive oil and lemon dressing. Then a small piece of smoked salmon or cold pork or chicken. I drink water followed by tea with skimmed milk. It is not difficult, but neither is it particularly pleasant.

The only perk I am allowed is a snack of root vegetables as I have decided to steer clear of fruit and tomatoes altogether. I am not entirely sure why, but I get the impression that anything with sugar is bad news, and carrots in particular are a no-go area. Dinner is the one meal that I do look forward to, and by early afternoon I am already salivating at the thought of the piece of meat or game that I am going to cook – with lentils, mixed with onions, garlic, carrots and celery all browned in oil and cooked in chicken stock for approximately 20–25 minutes. I use this method for pearl barley and quinoa, too, and then, sometimes skipping the no-sugar rule, I might have an apple for pudding. As the days and nights get colder I make myself Tom Yum soup, a hot and warming beverage with absolutely no nutritional value.

But, as I quickly learnt from Rose, the essential thing about food is the portions. They are tiny, and are helped through the system by packets of Senokot and other laxatives, a tip I was given by one of the lads. Life on the loo becomes a little more comfortable but I am now coming to grips with, and have a better understanding of, what wasting jockeys go through in their day-to-day existence. They do this every day with very little let-up, and real respect to them for what they put themselves through to do the job they love.

With little time left, ideally I have to lose another five pounds, maybe a bit more to factor in the extra weight for the back protector, which all jockeys must wear, boots and the saddle. I suspect that the extremes of this diet are starting to play with my mental health as I have started becoming prone to peculiar bouts of depression, as well as getting increasingly paranoid and obsessed about my weight loss. Getting onto my feet for the first time I doubt whether I can do it. I just want it to be over. This is how I feel from time to time. I want my life back. At other times I don't and I convince myself that I want to stay at Heads Farm, doing what I'm doing, for ever.

On Thursday morning, as the string is descending the steep track towards the gallops on the other side of the Wantage road, and just as we are about to cross what is quite a dangerous corner in the road, a driver comes haring round the bend. He is going so fast that he has difficulty keeping the car upright on the bend and immediately sees the string of horses ahead of him. He brakes hard, skids out of control, hits the hedge to his right and punctures both front tyres. There are huge, long, ingrained skid marks down the road. The screech of the tyres is horrible. The string of horses rears up, runs backwards and for a second I think there is going to be a horrible, terrible, bloodbath. How there isn't I shall never know. Nobody falls off, not one of the brave, Trojan horsemen hits the turf, but we are all very shaken by it and talk of little else as we continue on our way.

The vast majority of drivers couldn't give a fuck about horses. They see them simply as animals that are in the way, to be passed, overtaken, ignored, even hit. In 2006 there were more than 3,000 road accidents involving horses, and three human fatalities. The same year a drunken driver hurtling down the road that divides Newmarket Heath hit one of Sir Mark Prescott's horses. Maunik, suffering terrible injuries, was put down the following day, when he should have been running in his first race.

The ironic thing about the West Berkshire countryside is that, while the surroundings are magnificent, this seems to have escaped the attention of many of those who live closest to it. Hares and deer run wild, partridge rise and fly low across the grass downland, frightened in the wake of the red kites that soar high above us in the sky. The hedges are neat and well trimmed, the ancient turf lovingly tended. It is a place of great beauty. But each time we ride out to the gallops across the Great Shefford to Wantage road and pass from one part of Charlie's land to another, we find litter strewn everywhere. Between the two utilitarian white-painted cottages that are set just back from the road, every morning there is some new bit of rubbish blowing about or lying in the gardens: a McDonald's bag and wrapper, a newspaper, numerous plastic bottles, all despoiling the landscape. None of the lads seems remotely concerned by this even though the paper blows under the horses' legs, giving them a serious dose of the heebie-jeebies. Whoever lives in these houses is clearly quite well off. A gleaming red Mercedes sits outside one and yet the litter blows here, there and everywhere. No one picks it up or clears it away. After several weeks into this, I went up on the gallops with Charlie to watch some horses work and as we came down I got him to stop the car, dashed out and collected all the rubbish. By the time I had finished the back of the car was, if not brimming, still pretty full with the filth and muck that the good burghers of Berkshire had chosen to discard by the wayside. Although Charlie agrees with my sentiments and rantings about the litter, once I have filled his car with the filth and crap he stares at me as if to say, 'You really are mad, aren't you?'

Between training there is little to occupy the lads other than watching the Racing Channel on Sky, and Eldiiar has run into trouble yet again. It turns out that he spent the previous evening putting away a skinful of vodka and beer before clambering into his uninsured car, which he promptly overturned in one of Charlie's fields, this despite Albert telling him not to drive under any circumstances. The advice went unheeded and most of the morning was spent working out how to get his car out of the field without alerting the police. As we are ambling down towards the gallops I mention to Eldiiar that if he had knocked down my thirteen-year-old son, or anyone else for that matter, he would have been in serious trouble. The whole thing goes over his head and he says if the police come to get him he'll go back to Kazakhstan. When I tell him, quite seriously, that I would come and hunt him down if he had injured my son, he turns to me with a look of complete contempt and says, 'I don't care, I not frightened, I not frightened of anyone, Mr Boss Dominic', as he always refers to me. With a temperament like this it is unlikely that he will ever become a jockey. I know he is taking the piss, thinking, 'who is this four-eyed bloke who was once fat and is a friend of the guv'nor?' We trot on and I am still seething at him, because, as charming as he can be, he is extremely hot-headed, and it is no wonder that Trigger is always watching him out of the corner of his eye.

Chapter Fourteen

With only a few days to go, one of Charlie's professional jockeys, Jimmy McCarthy, comes to Heads Farm to ride a pricey purchase that Charlie has just made. He is to run at Ascot. While he is there he gives me some sound advice about how I need to deal with Dancing Marabout, with so little time to go before the race. Jimmy is a great smoker and coffee drinker, and in the stables he talks me through the final preparations he puts his horses through. The butterflies are already fluttering around my stomach. 'Come on then, let's see how you ride,' says Jimmy and we head out to the gallops so that he can put me through my paces. I may not look it, but I feel like a prize-fighter in the last days before the big fight.

We box five horses up to Compton Down and this time I sit in the back of a huge, gleaming horse transporter, with John from Walworth and Nicky, an old and experienced hand. Nicky has worked with horses his whole life, temporarily giving it up to work in a warehouse in Wantage, but found he couldn't keep away from them, so now he rides out for Charlie most mornings. John, who knows more about horses than I ever will, sits there calmly. He has done this hundreds of times and doesn't understand why I am making such a fuss about it, as I sit nervously chewing my nails. We unload and the driver of the horse lorry legs us all up. Dancing Marabout is full of himself and when we trot, then canter, I find it tricky to control him, until we finally slow at the top of the hill before circling for the return. Trigger then gives me an almighty bollocking and says that I was 'weaving' during the canter, 'first right then left. You were all over the fucking place, your reins were too tight so he was fighting for his head all the time, it was dangerous. If that happens on the day you'll kill someone. You must keep a straight course.' Trigger is right, as always. Keeping a straight course is a hard and fast rule in horse racing. Jockeys who don't keep a straight course get into serious trouble with the stewards.

As we descend the hill to where we jump off, Charlie gives me my instructions. 'Just sit in beside Jimmy and Nicky, don't overtake them but get off swiftly and go when they go. If he's pulling too hard pass them by but tell them you're coming, shout out. But then when you get to the mile pole try and overtake them, go for it then.'

He jumps off, but too soon, because the rest of them are miles away, but I can't stop him. I had left the start too long and within a couple of strides I realize that he just wants to be in the front. With Charlie's last words ringing in my ears, trying to ride as close to Jimmy's arse is a lost one, as Dancing Marabout whooshes off ahead of the others. Not only that, but my steering is all over the place, and for the first time in a long while I get quite scared.

The idea is that we stick between clearly defined furlong pegs. The trouble is that, because on the day I will not be allowed to wear glasses, I am not wearing them today either. This means that I can't see the furlong pegs and I have to follow the hoof prints in the ground where other horses have gone before. Added to this is the fact that it is absolutely tipping down with rain and I have to keep my eyes as tightly closed as possible to protect them from the rain as I am not wearing goggles either. By the third marker we are so wide that I have to haul Dancing Marabout in and he jumps over the peg. But on we go, and there's not another horse in sight. I daren't look behind me, and, although I know what Trigger is going to say to me when we get back, I settle down and try to enjoy myself while it lasts.

By now, Dancing Marabout is using every last bit of energy and muscle to keep up the tempo, and we are really motoring. As we near the top of the hill there is a fence made from tape and wire that runs from across the horizon, with a gap in it of maybe 20 feet in length. I have to get through that gap but he is belting along so quickly and the rain is lashing down so hard that I cannot see the gap and we are heading straight for the fence. If I can only see the gap in the fence we'll be all right but I can't see the gap and it flashes through my mind that we are going to get tangled up in the tape. Thoughts of Zachariah in Ireland come to mind, then I haul him right-handed and pick up the tracks that have gone before and we are OK again.

As we hit the mile marker – nothing more than a length of track crossing the course on top of the downs – he is straightening up and keeps a steady line. My feet are soaked through from the rain and frozen solid in the November air, and my cheeks are streaming, but the only thing I can feel is the exhilaration of the animal beneath me. He is giving it everything he has, and his coat is steaming in the rain from the heat pouring from his body. I realize that at this stage I am little more than a passenger. With four furlongs to go, this would be about the time that Cote Soleil would have started to slow considerably, needing to be egged on to cross the finishing line. Not so Dancing Marabout, who just keeps pulling at the bit, telling me he knows what he is doing, even if I don't, and at just three years old. As we near the end of the gallop I make a lame effort to slow him down. As we pass Charlie, who is sitting behind the wheel of his car, Jimmy comes up on my left-hand side, perfectly in control and in overdrive. He just eats up the ground and is two lengths in front of me before I realize what is happening. I had the beating of him for nearly a mile and a half and then, as if by magic, like a rocket he is past me. He'd been sitting in behind me, perfectly in control, just waiting for the moment, the second, when he'd say 'off you go' to Freeze the Flame. And he does. His horse is working away beneath him, like a duck scarpering from a pond. The legs are doing all the work and Jimmy just sits there, calmly, beautifully, helping, not hampering, the horse below him. When we pull up I am emotionally exhausted. As we walk back to the lorry I ask Trigger how, on a scale of one to ten, I have done. 'If one is the tops and ten's the bottom, you scored eleven,' he says and laughs. Charlie comes up beside us in the jeep and asks how we all got on. He particularly asks me if I am all right, as if he's expecting me to break down and scream that I can't do it, can't race, that the experience has frayed my nerves for good. I am all right, a bit shaken by the speed of it all, perhaps, but I am determined to get to Towcester. He mumbles to Trigger about getting a stronger bit for Thursday so that the steering and the brakes might work a little better. Trigger says something but it is indistinct so I have no idea what form of bit and bridle my wet, puffed-out horse will be wearing come Towcester. But then, recalling my previous conversation with Charlie, I consider that I don't actually want a stronger bit. The whole point about the race-horse is that he is trained to go forward at the fastest possible speed, not jib and ball up his power but to go forward and expend it.

We meander back to the lorry and Trigger tells me where I went wrong. 'You were miles behind them when the others jumped off, so he was mad keen to get in front. You should have been right up with Jimmy, right up Jimmy's arse, from the very beginning. That's why you got in the mess you got in. Don't worry, though,' he adds, 'it happens to the best jockeys sometimes.' I think to myself that it does indeed happen to the best jockeys but that is probably by design and not by accident. Making sure a favourite doesn't win at the behest of a bookmaker can be and is a very profitable little sideline that some jockeys indulge in. Trigger can see that I am a bit down in the mouth about the workout and the balls-up I made of it. And what a mess it was. Out of control, unable to see as the rain and wind pounded out of the sky and incapable of either steering or stopping. It was not the best preparation for Towcester and serious doubts begin to devour me about my capabilities. If the horse did this on a work ride, what the hell was he going to do when we got to Towcester?

I returned to London that afternoon very dejected after what should have been the perfect final preparation for the race. Driving along the M4 on the way home I started making up excuses for why I couldn't ride on Thursday. They ranged from a bad bout of the flu to the wackier idea of engineering a fall from a horse in order to break an arm or leg which, by now, I had convinced myself I was going to do on the day anyway.

At least this way people would say 'he tried'. Then I thought of all the hours of effort and pain and suffering that everyone had put in to try and get me to the racetrack. The sacrifice Rose and the children had made, me not being with them for weeks on end. I'd also raised more than £5,000 for the Spinal Injuries charity. I had just sent out a round-robin e-mail soliciting funds and what was pretty amazing was that 95 per cent of those I'd e-mailed immediately pledged money. It came in from everywhere. The biggest donation was £500, the smallest £5, but it gave me a huge amount of satisfaction just knowing that there were people out there who liked me enough to support the cause. But I would, of course, only see the money if I got round. By the time I opened the front door in London my conviction had been restored. I was definitely going. I couldn't let them down. Not Rose or the children or Charlie or Trigger or Albert or John, or all the other countless individuals who'd helped me get this far.

* * *

On the Saturday evening we had a party in London for Bonfire Night. An army of children and adults turned up to feast on Rose's cuisine. I sat at the head of the table chewing on a piece of celery and drinking pint after pint of water as I watched the assembled company wolf ham and cheese and bread and pickles and Stockbridge sausages. The strange thing is I didn't have the slightest inclination to join them. I was entirely focused on losing weight, strengthening thigh muscles, triceps and biceps, and was very glad when they all finally left so that I could retire to bed. On the table in front of me lay a plate with a few sticks of celery, some radishes and broccoli – all raw. There was also a jug of water. While the others feasted I contentedly fasted. My determination was absolute, and I overheard people whispering to each other that they thought I was not right, that the whole 'horse thing' had gone a bit too far. After all, it was just a race, wasn't it? I knew they could not properly understand, so I did my best to talk about it as little as possible.

In the kitchen on that cold Saturday night in November the environment felt totally and utterly alien. This was my life as it had once been lived, not as I was living it now. I had a very strong inkling that I was in the wrong place. I wanted to go out and have a chat with Dancing Marabout. I wanted to get up in the morning and go and ride him but it wasn't going to happen, not tonight at least. So, before the children woke up, I slipped out of the house the following morning, having packed my bags for the final trip to Heads Farm. The next time I saw them would be at Towcester.

I do not see Charlie all day until we sit down together for dinner that night in the kitchen. Ordinarily it would just have been the two of us having dinner, but tonight, Josef, he who had no front teeth, who gave up believing in God and instead turned to horses when his mother died, has joined us. As well as being a good rider and a talented horseman, Josef drives Charlie to the races whenever he has a runner, and is indispensable to the running of the stables. They make a fantastic double act. I once suggested to Josef that Bianca would make a good girlfriend or partner for Charlie. 'You joking, she so fit she kill him and we have no boss left if you do that. If Bianca and Charles "do it" there is then no more Charles,' he said, bursting into peals of laughter.

Although I've drunk nothing for weeks, that night I decide that I should join the pair of them, so we sit up drinking Famous Grouse and Armagnac and smoking Marlboro Reds. Josef keeps saying to me 'no more, no more' when I offer him another drink. But of course he relents, about five times that evening, and we have a great laugh and he tells me the story about Digger Boy, a horse Charlie used to train.

During November 2006 he ran at Taunton. Not only did he not perform, falling at the beginning of his race, but like many horses continued in the race jockeyless. Instead of pulling up, as most horses eventually do, he kept up with the leader all the way round, niggling at him and taking every fence with him. He kept up with him until two from home when he lunged at the jockey, clasping the jockey's elbow between his teeth and trying to pull him off his horse. Digger Boy wouldn't give up, and Josef grabbed hold of my arm as he showed me just how hard the horse had clamped the jockey as he tried to pull him off backwards. Josef used to ride Digger Boy and as he's telling me this story a tear comes to his eye. He thought that Digger Boy's efforts on behalf of another horse were heroic, the idea that he wanted to protect another horse a noble one. Josef told me that Digger Boy did in fact manage to pull the jockey off and he seemed rather pleased at the outcome. The race was eventually won by a filly called Park Lane Princess, the favourite. When, much later, I asked Josef what had become of Digger Boy, he feigned ignorance. Perhaps he thought the story revealed too much about his feelings for his horses, something that he wanted to keep private, something that he only felt able to expand upon when he was 'in the drink'.

* * *

It is our final gallop, the last chance for me to correct any problems with my technique as we are only going for a gentle canter on the gallops. The petulance of Saturday has completely gone. Dancing Marabout pulls up very nicely at the end of the gallops. I ride two more and then go back to the kitchen at Heads Farm before running a bath. My nerves are starting to fray and I am having trouble concentrating. The pre-race nerves have kicked in already, not helped by Albert who keeps teasing me in front of the lads. 'I tell you something, you'll be shitting yerself in a couple of days. Up there on his back before the race you won't be able to do anything you'll be that fookin' nervous.'

I try to ignore Albert by laughing it off, but I know that he's right. To take my mind of it I walk out into the yard once we have scrubbed the horses down and stand looking over the end of the door into his stables. I want to see if I can, Dr Doolittle-like, decipher what is going on in his head. There he is, in his box. Tiny, golden in colour and good-natured. His rugs are a bit crooked so I walk into his box and straighten them up on his quarters, pat him and kiss his neck. He doesn't lift a leg, or show his teeth, or lay his ears flat back on his neck. He's just calm and collected. That's it. We're ready. I fill up his bucket with water and close the door behind me.

I returned to the house and decided to head off to Wantage to weigh myself one last time. According to Boots' weighing machine I am 12 stone 2lb with a day to go until my race. As I get near to Boots, a man passes me eating a croissant filled with cheese and ham. I become obsessed with it and want to – and very nearly do – stop the man eating it and ask him for a bite. It doesn't even look that nice, but I want a bite. Just one. And then I shake myself out of it, walk into the news-agent, buy sixty cigarettes, cross the street to the health food shop and buy numerous packets of pulses, pearl barley, lentils, quinoa and enough salad for the final assault on my rapidly depleting girth.

As the sky darkens outside I try to distract myself by read-ing the accounts of the great jockeys in whose footsteps I am trying to follow. But it is no use and I can't help but imagine what it would be like to have five, six or seven horses crash down on top of me. Three quarters of a ton at 30 mph will surely snap my spine, at the very least break limbs. The smash-ups recorded in the Heads Farm accident book come back into focus, so too my long chat with the seriously bashed up and battered Shane Kelly and the horrible, debilitating injuries suffered by so many jockeys. They are nightmarish thoughts of spending the rest of my life in a wheelchair. I am now exactly the same age my father was when he ended up in a wheelchair.

It seems that someone somewhere does not want me to race at all. In the evening of our final rehearsal, while I am preparing dinner, Charlie comes in after evening stables and says that Dancing Marabout is seriously lame, and for half a second I think that this is the excuse not to ride that I have been looking for. Albert had spotted that he had a corn on his foot while he was circling around his box in some discomfort. The farrier, who puts on the shoes and takes them off the horse, came, lanced the corn and a huge splattering of pus, blood and gunge squirted out. There is absolutely no way that this horse is going to be ready for the race. Charlie sort of pats me on the back and says, 'Don't worry. If you get there you get there, if you don't you don't.' They are wise words but that is not the way I have ever looked at things.

Each day Albert expertly poultices the foot and washes and disinfects it every few hours. Albert truly is a saint, but even he is not sure what will happen. By Wednesday morning Albert has put the crippled Dancing Marabout on the horse walker and, fifteen minutes later, I am up there on his back giving him a slow canter around the field. It seems highly improbable, but we are back in business. Charlie treats the entire episode in a very matter-of-fact way, an attitude, Albert tells me, that comes from his having seen this kind of thing happen many times before. For the first time, though, as the race was hanging in the balance, I get a real sense that Trigger, John and Eldiiar, on the other hand, are very anxious that this once fat bloke who, three months earlier, could hardly sit on a horse and who can now ride pretty well, should have his day at the races. This is not to say that Charlie doesn't care. I know he does, but this is a tiny race, not the type of race he is used to, nor the type he particularly wants to be involved with. He'd much rather be at Royal Ascot or Goodwood or the Derby, and who can blame him?

Chapter Fifteen

The night before the race, an old friend, Ian Bent, from the BBC in Manchester, who has come to do a radio programme on the race, arrives at Heads Farm to meet Charlie and the lads.

I show Ian around the yard, and introduce him to Charlie and the equine inmates. He goes to his room, unpacks, has a bath and we all sit down in the kitchen. Charlie is a wonderful host. Ian, a Mancunian liberal, is enquiring and, I think, pretty knocked out by what he finds. A rather eccentric Old Etonian racehorse trainer is not perhaps what he is used to, and he realizes that the horse world is not just filled with toffs from old money, but that they are extremely generous and welcoming people – at least I think that's what he thinks, but there's no real telling with Ian because he keeps his cards very close to his chest. Workwise he tells you everything, but his private thoughts he keeps to himself; they are his own. But on his stable tour he takes a real interest; although a world away from the North, he laps up what he is presented with. I never found out what Ian thought about Charlie or Heads Farm. I never asked him. He is sport mad and the horse is a great leveller of people. Although, ultimately I thought he probably disapproved he only ever showed encouragement.

I cook chicken and barley for the three of us while Charlie produces a bottle of his best claret for Ian, who drinks the lot himself as Charlie has reverted to one of his more traditional diets. I dare not go to Wantage to weigh myself any longer but I know that I'm within three or four pounds of the requisite weight. So I make do with water, green tea and tiny portions of chicken and salad. Before going to bed I have a final crap and lose another pound.

In the morning I sense that this is going to be a good news day. I spring out of bed at five, knowing that the day of reckoning is twelve hours closer. The first thing I do after getting up, brushing up, eating breakfast and swigging Earl Grey is get into the car with Charlie and Ian and head off to Lambourn where the great AP is doing some schooling for Charlie. It's dark and cold but there he is – the Corinthian himself, ready and waiting, all sinews and adrenalin. AP has driven over in a gleaming black Audi, a testament to the fact that serious money can be made by the very best jockeys. Gazing through the darkened windows I note that there are packets of chewing gum and cans of Red Bull on the back seat to suppress the appetite, something that is familiar to every jockey, at whatever level. The lads who ride the horses up here for Charlie are in awe of AP McCoy, champion jockey for the last fifteen consecutive seasons and a man who is without doubt the most successful jump jockey of all time – ever. And he in turn is so polite, so nice and full of encouragement for the lads that it very nearly makes me weep. If you are an aspiring jockey, talking to and receiving advice from McCoy is similar to a young footballer receiving advice from Pelé, David Beckham, Maradona or Kaká; it cannot be bettered. There is no one like AP and his generosity of spirit just envelopes me.

Once he has answered all the questions the lads have for him, explained what they should and shouldn't do with particular horses, he turns his attention to the once fat bloke with glasses, nervously standing at the back, waiting his turn. I am buzzing with all sorts of questions that I want to ask him about the races of his that I have watched, but there are really only two questions that I need him to answer: what tactics should I employ? How should I ride the race?

'Well,' says AP, referring to Dancing Marabout, who he knows well. 'He won't be the quickest fellow in the world, and you haven't picked the easiest racetrack either. Towcester is a bit of a bastard.' I think to myself that, actually AP, he felt like the quickest horse in the universe when he ran off with me on Saturday. We also talk about hitting the horse, the thing that all good jockeys must learn to do on the run-in to the finishing post. There comes a moment in every race when the horse is so knackered that they want to give up, but the stick helps to encourage them to give that one last push for the finish line. The great man surprises me. 'Don't hit him, don't even think about it, you'll unbalance him and you'll unbalance yourself. Don't do it, don't even carry a stick.'

As for Towcester being 'a bit of a bastard', everyone has told me about the final uphill sprint, but with so little time left there is not a moment to think about it as we make the final preparations. I have never been to the course, so I have no idea what is in store for me. As AP drives off, wishing me luck, I go into something of a daze.

After all the doubts and all the years of waiting, the big event is just hours away. In around six hours I'll be up there on Dancing Marabout's back, ready to race.

On the way back from Lambourn, Charlie gives instructions. He is very nervous about me crashing into the heels of another horse in front. He is also nervous that the horse is going to run off with me, before running out of steam and then be too knackered to get up the hill. He is so nervous, in fact, that he decides he has to go to another race meeting with an owner so as not to witness the horror of what is about to unfold at Towcester.

One of my final duties before packing my bags is to do an interview for Radio 4's Today programme, which had sent a radio car to Heads Farm earlier in the morning. Marcus Armytage, a *Daily Telegraph* contributor, and a man who rode the winner of the 1990 Grand National, is a co-interviewee.

He tells me that my legs are going to be 'like jelly' once I've come up the hill at Towcester, but that there is a great atmosphere at the course, so I should enjoy it enormously. Afterwards, like a forgetful old man, I begin packing my bags. I tick everything off: breeches, hat, stick (which will not be needed), vest, back protector and boots. My valet in the weighing room will have my silks, the blue colours of Charlie's stables I am to ride in, and my saddle. I also stuff the bag with six bottles of Lucozade sports drink and a packet of jelly babies. The last piece of advice AP gave me was to start chewing them like mad and drink Lucozade after I had been weighed out in order to artificially rev up my energy levels, which will by then be at an all-time low.

There are lots of messages of good wishes on the phone and loads on the computer. An old friend, Peter Robinson, himself a horse enthusiast and one of the luckiest owners around, sends only an image of a wolf sitting on its haunches, howling at the moon.

My nerve finally breaks and I ask Charlie about the possibility of a stronger bit for Dancing Marabout, along the lines of something that cowboys might have used to control their mounts. All he says is that 'the idea is to get them to go forward; we don't really want to rig him up with a gag snaffle now, do we? We don't want to stop him going forward. He is a racehorse after all.' Of course Charlie is right and it dawns on me yet again what a very different proposition a racehorse is to a riding horse, a hunter, a show hack or a pony. This is an entirely different game with speed, ferocity and brutality at its heart. The racehorse is here so that men and women, from the breeders to the owners to the jockeys and the man in the street wagering his £1 bet on the outcome of the Epsom Derby can, for one moment, dream of glory. It strikes me that in many ways this race is not really about me at all, but about the bookmakers, the saddlers, farriers, stable lads, teachers, racecourse managers – everyone who has anything at all to do with the horse. I am merely a passenger.

By 11.30 a.m. the final preparations have been made, and Dancing Marabout is boxed up and heading off with John in a big gleaming horsebox. He looks fine. He's been brushed and combed and is shining in his skin. Once we are sure that nothing has been left behind, Ian and I get into the car as the fog descends and we make our way to Towcester. The drive takes just short of two hours, and we bounce along the A roads out of Berkshire and into the roads and lanes of Oxfordshire and finally Northamptonshire. We are like a couple of grumpy old men discussing the state of the nation, grumbling about the usual issues of two men in midlife: the state of the BBC, the difficulties of bringing up children, food, stupidity, the age of celebrity. We talk about almost everything except the race, and, although he has asked me about life at Heads Farm and Dancing Marabout, it is only when we arrive at Towcester that I realize Ian has very cleverly distracted me from talking or thinking about what I am up against, what I am about to embark upon.

Towcester is like no other racecourse that I have ever been to. The sheer size of it is daunting, for a start. On arrival, three hours before my race, I am overcome by the enormity of the stand with its huge towers, which remind me of Churchill Downs in Kentucky where I watched a horse called Ferdinand win the 1987 Kentucky Derby. I had been sent out to cover it for the now defunct *Today* newspaper twenty-one years ago. For what is essentially a country racecourse, the stands and buildings on the course are very garish, crude and large – perhaps this reflects an American influence on the Hesketh family who own the course.

And then I see the track with the final, Herculean hill that runs up to the finishing post. I know it is going to be tough, but this is something else. I watch a few races and seeing those horses staggering up the hill, sweat and blood and mud everywhere, finally brings home to me the enormity of my task.

Just as I am about to start hyperventilating with nervousness, I spot Jack, Lara and Rose, who started it all, and I fancy that she is beginning to regret she ever encouraged the idea in the first place. Their presence adds a certain poignance, as does that of my mother since it was she who first put me on the back of a horse. There are old friends, too. Emma, who taught me what horses meant to me when we were both only schoolchildren; and Ralph, for whom I bought his first pony when he was twelve. Eileen, who I helped on the road back to riding with the purchase of two horses called Mr TK and Barney, has come all the way over from Suffolk to be here with her father. A little later I see that Keith, who unwittingly embroiled me in everything that is Ireland and horses, has

made it, too, along with Danny, who I introduced to racehorse ownership. He's talking to George, who set me off on
this venture by letting me ride Daz. In fact, almost everyone
who has been part of my life as a horse lover is here, and I am
in danger of overloading the occasion with significance.

It is cold and at the allotted time of 2.30 I meet at the
weighing room to walk the course. Only no one is there. The
weighing room manager, a gentle old man who looks like he
has worked here forever, says he thinks everyone has left. He
tells me to cross over into the middle of the track and ask his
driver to drop me round to where the group are walking the
course. I run, stagger, across the track, look down the hill and
feel the turf beneath my feet. I am extremely nervous; I have
missed the bus. Where was I when the other riders were
assembling? This is not what I expected at all. I thought it
would all be a lot easier and walking the course on a cold and
wet November afternoon instils no confidence in me whatsoever. This is the ground I am going to get Dancing Marabout
to run on in less than forty-five minutes and it is cut up like
ribbons, and in some places boggy with bare mud showing
through the grass after a full afternoon of racing on it. I refuse
to wear glasses even for this, so what I see while walking the
course is what I'll see when I'm riding it. Even in the last nine
months my sight has got worse and I regret not having had
my eyes laser-zapped. Contact lenses would have been a
happy medium. All I can think is 'Thank God the rails are
white'.

Tanya Sherwood, the wife of Oliver Sherwood, a trainer
who has entered two horses in the race, walks me round the
course. She could not be more helpful, or calming. While she
tries to settle my rapidly fraying nerves she points out where
the ground is heaviest and the bends that I will have to watch,

and she gives me a quick explanation of how I should ride them. The light is disappearing quickly, and with the wind whistling in the trees and the echo from the grandstand reverberating around the ground, I am half expecting a villain to jump out of the undergrowth and cosh me over the head, like they do in the best Dick Francis novels. By this time I am completely overcome by the task in hand, and the adrenalin has been pumping around my body for so long that I am slowly getting more and more tired. The crowd is vast, in part because a policy of free admission to the course has doubled the numbers in recent years. The course director realized that if you let the punters in for nothing you'd get more of them since they'd be more inclined to spend lots of money, so your takings in the restaurants, bars, hot dog stalls and what have you would all increase exponentially. And so they did at Towcester, and quite dramatically. In the first year of the experiment turnover doubled and profits were up by nearly the same amount. You might think that if every racecourse in the country did that then racing might save itself from oblivion, but it hasn't taken off widely just yet.

We return to the paddocks and I catch up briefly with all those who have come to watch, although I can hardly maintain my concentration. I talk, and hope, and feel my ribs and push in my stomach, thinking that this might help lighten the load ever so slightly. Photographers from local papers then ask to take pictures and to talk to me and interview me about motivation and the horse and Charlie and my life. I can barely stand still, but it does succeed in distracting me, momentarily, from the enormity of the task before me. The call then goes up for all jockeys to ready themselves and I edge towards the controlled area of the weighing room. There's no backing out, not now, not ever.

The weighing room resembles something from Bedlam. Intrinsically, like everything to do with horse racing, it is very well organized. The jockeys' valets in their claret-coloured aprons are cleaning and polishing and scrubbing boots and saddles and silks and shouting out for saddles and boots and goggles and silks. But here, today, time is not on their side. There is a race every thirty minutes and we are ushered through by the officials who make sure the jockeys present themselves at the right weight, in the right kit to the clerk of the scales, who I hope will weigh me out, saddle and all, at 12 stone dead.

There are two young Irish lads, both of them clearly in great pain. One is having his collar bone reset and the other is having a large gash above his eyebrow stitched up, and there is a fair amount of blood. Some of the jockeys are wandering around naked, one with his huge member swinging from side to side like a limp truncheon. He is completely oblivious to the girls walking up to the scales and just carries on towelling himself down. Some of the jockeys gather round the TV screens to watch the racing from other courses. 'He's pulling it, he's fooking pulled him, look at the cunt,' bellows one at the TV screen as he watches another jockey on a far-away course racing, perhaps not as hard as he might. As I enter the changing room to get ready all the jockeys gaze at me in disbelief. I can see exactly what they are thinking – what on earth is someone like him doing here? But now I am as anxious as they are to carry on and to ride in the next race, my race.

Only I have no kit, no saddle and the silk for the helmet is too small. John, known to all the valets, has not delivered the requisite gear. One valet gets out a pair of scissors and is about to split Charlie's beautiful, glorious silk up the back to ram it down onto the riding helmet. I wonder what my dad is thinking about the helmet; it appears to have the biggest and best British Kitemark for safety emblazoned on it. I am sure he would have approved.

The valet manages to find a silk that doesn't need to be torn or cut to make it fit. He gets it around the helmet and I edge towards the scales with my tiny slip of a saddle that John has finally delivered to the weighing room under my arm. I take the step up and am weighed both manually and digitally. The scales say 12 stone 2lb. After nine months of gruelling regime change I will be riding with two pounds overweight and I feel a bit stupid. Although I am well under 12 stone naked, having tipped the Wantage scales at 11 stone 10 the previous day, the boots, body protector and helmet add perhaps six. So, for the first time in my adult life, I am under 12 stone but if only I could have shed that extra two pounds. In a horse race it means everything, as I am about to find out.

Once the weighing out has been done there is nothing left but to sit and wait for the bell signalling the moment that we have to mount up. I start to cram my mouth full of jelly babies and gulp down Lucozade. I can feel the energy rushing through my blood, but rather than just giving me an energy boost it makes me slightly manic. What have I agreed to do? As I exit the weighing room, Ralph turns to me and says, 'Remember what I told you when you were waiting for Rose in the church? I said it wasn't too late to back out. That is the same now. No one will think any the worse of you.' It is getting dark very quickly and I am cold and alone; photographers are milling around. Reporters keep asking me questions about my motives. Ian shoves a microphone under my nose and I am unable to say anything, I just jangle with nerves. Ten minutes to go.

As I walk to the parade ring there is John, all jolly and full of 'cor blimey' expressions, telling me not to worry and just nudging me along with encouragement. I'm half thinking that John didn't tell me enough, possibly didn't want to, about the ordered life of racing – where you pick your kit up from, where your saddle is going to be, the things that made me nervous in the weighing room.

Rose and Jack and Lara are waiting for me outside the changing room doors, and, while they can see that I am as nervous as hell, they put on brave smiles. I give Jack, who is nearly as big as me now and twice as strong, a big hug and he tries to push a folded piece of paper into my hand. He wants me to open it and read it and I am afraid. Inexplicably, I push it away and give it back to him, telling him to hold onto it, that I'll read it later. It is the wrong thing to do, and I can see that he is disappointed and downhearted at my snub. After all, he's hardly seen me for three months. I make a promise to myself to make it up to him when all this is over.

I make my way to meet John who is leading the horse round. Dancing Marabout is fidgety and excitable. 'Don't worry, he'll look after you, you'll be all right just as long as you do what the guv'nor said.' Then Dancing Marabout, full of the occasion, starts jiggling around. He's been through this before and I haven't, so I try not to get spooked when he starts dancing from side to side as we make our way down to the start line. We're here. At last.

After a false start when I miss the rhythm of the heave into the saddle, John legs me up on board. As my bottom touches down on the saddle, my nerves get the better of me and I try to control myself by taking deep breaths. I pat the horse's neck and try to calm him and John says soothing words into his ear. But once I am up there I am surprisingly calm, full of equine morphine and not nearly as nervous as I was in the changing room, as though some of Dancing Marabout's composure has rubbed off on me. As John leads us out onto the track we both start getting over-excited, and John keeps telling me to loosen my reins as he keeps a firm grasp on Dancing Marabout. The clock on the stadium tower has just struck 4.30 and it is now very dark indeed, the dampness of this cold November afternoon closing in on us. I can barely see a thing other than the white of the railings. It is the last race of the day, and if we don't get started soon they are going to have to call it off. The commentator, who clearly knows nothing of my journey here, announces that 'the Charlie Egerton-trained Dancing Marabout with Dominic Prince up is the clear favourite at 5-2'. I can only assume that all the friends who have come to see me have plundered all their hard-earned onto the tiny slip of a horse and me.

Those words from the commentator are the last I remember before the official starter drops his flag and we are off, just the two of us, alone in the freezing Northamptonshire landscape pitted against another nine horses and their jockeys. The last thought that goes through my head is that I have done everything I want to do in life apart from this. While I know it is unlikely that anything really seriously bad is going to happen, it is, nevertheless, a distinct possibility. There are thousands of pounds of horseflesh waiting to crash down upon me and the one thing I do know is that the amateurs are the ones who get it, who are much more likely to be injured and maimed than the professionals.

I take the inside rail and try not to pull at Dancing Marabout's mouth. I slacken the reins, let them run through my hands and let him have a bit of head. I follow what we had practised over and over again and let him stretch his neck,

Jumbo to Jockey

and try not to stifle him with the reins. He responds by moving along beautifully underneath me, keeping to a soft, gentle rhythm. I can hear Trigger's voice in the back of my mind telling me not to give him too much for fear that he might run away with me. He takes a big pull and finds his own pace, but before we have reached the first turn he has already settled and is puffing and blowing happily.

We start to move slowly through the field. As we take the first bend I look around me at the other jockeys, almost none of whom have ridden a race before either. Although my vision is blurred without my glasses I can still see that they are all looking as frightened and as worried as I am feeling. We are all in this together. We career down the hill and there is a girl on my left, clearly completely out of control, and I try and give her as wide a berth as possible, terrified of what might happen otherwise. We take the right-hand bend at the bottom of the hill and Dancing Marabout momentarily loses his footing, his off-side shoulder drops as the ground underneath him falls away, and he stumbles. Behind me are five huge horses which will be unable to avoid me if we do fall and I can already picture them squashing me to death, or leaving me with a broken neck for good measure. But Dancing Marabout regains his footing and I keep my balance and on we hurtle.

Halfway around the course, the track flattens out again. This is where AP told me to take a breath, 'let the horse take a breather and fill your own lungs with air along the straight, because you'll need it as you round the bend and head for home'. So, on we gallop, the horse under me, paddling away, the steady clomping of the hooves in the mud the only sound I can hear above the wind whistling in my ears. Although I was told not to look over my shoulder I do glance to my left and right and there are horses all around me. I am still just ahead of all but one of them. I'm standing up tall in the stir-rups and I can feel what taut, strong calf muscles I have. I don't feel tired, or breathless, just joyous. Dancing Marabout is stretching his neck and I can see the sweat pouring from him and the smell of it mixes with the leather of the bridle and the sticky, slippery reins. He's now finding the going a little heavy, he's breathing hard, the spittle starting to foam at the corners of his mouth. The steering works beautifully, so I lean forward and whisper words of encouragement: 'Go on, my son,' I say, as we turn into the final quarter and the hill. At first he doesn't react, but then his ears start to twitch and I feel the reins tighten again. 'Come on, my son. Let's do it.' I'm still tucked pretty handily on the rails and the runaway horse on my left is flagging but up in his place comes another. Now there's one final exertion, the five furlongs up the hill and, as AP reminded me, I am about to find out that it is a 'bit of a bastard'. Fatally, because we are cruising along so merrily and I am having such a nice time with him behaving so well and not pulling at the reins, I momentarily lose concentration on keeping the reins tight. The moment I do he starts to slacken, the fatigue rising through his body no longer being countered by the adrenalin. With all fear extinguished, and all horror of potential damage and hurt gone, I drop my hands about two furlongs out while in second position. I had never imagined that either of us had the scope to be handily placed on this or any other course. At the start line I was happy just to get round in one piece and bring my little chestnut horse up the hill, all sweating and puffing and blowing, his mind completely on the job. But we had a chance to win it, and, through all my inexperience, we blew it. I was just frozen in amazement at what I had done, when in fact I was in the race with a real chance of winning.

By the time I realize what I have done it is too late. The horses that were behind me start coming at me thick and fast as we come up the hill and into the final turn. With no stick to encourage him I resort to shouting at him 'go on, go on'. I bellow it at the top of my voice, and I kick for home as I've never kicked. Now I'm screaming, shouting and egging him on. And then to my left I see the crowds all hollering and shouting and heaving their enthusiasm behind me. I can just about hear the individual words of encouragement as I push and squeeze and try to extract every last drop of effort out of the horse and myself. While 95 per cent of me is concentrating on getting him to finish as high up the order as possible, 5 per cent is tuning into the noise of the crowd, listening out for familiar voices. And I swear I can hear them all – Rose, the children, my mother, Emma, Ralph. The words of each of them carry through the air as I pass them in the last hundred metres to the finish line.

As I slid off his back a strange thing happened. I was ready for my legs to turn to jelly. But, as if by some miracle they did not wobble; instead they felt taut and strong, and I stood back down on earth trying to comprehend the huge ramifications of what I had just done. I had done it. I had realized a childhood dream. I had ridden my horse and come out of it alive.

I strode off to have my picture taken and then back to the weighing room. I was in a state of disbelief and then a message popped up on my mobile. It just said, 'Well done. Edgy'. It was from Charlie. Charles Ralph Egerton, the man who had facilitated my great dream, the man who has only ever wanted to train racehorses. The man I should perhaps have been. I had come fifth.

It was properly dark by the time I got out of the weighing room. The rain and the autumn skies had descended at a more rapid rate than anyone had expected, and with the darkness came the cold as I shivered in my silks. I climbed out of my boots, removed my hat and breeches and silks and breathed out deeply from the bottom of my lungs and from the bottom of my heart. For a moment I just stood in the changing room thinking about everyone who had made this possible, before shaking hands with all the officials, who had since learnt exactly why I was here. 'Well done. You looked like a pro.' I exchanged stories with the other riders as we got dressed before walking out of the weighing room, over to the bar and bought a huge glass of whisky, the first real alcohol I had drunk for three months – except, of course, for the slip the previous Sunday evening with Josef and Charlie.

A loud cheer went up as I entered the bar. For the next hour we stood around among the torn betting slips being swept up all around us and toasted the horse: 'To Dancing Marabout!' As we started to settle in, John said that we'd best get on the road, as we had a long drive back to Heads Farm. I had not seen Dancing Marabout since I had dismounted to be weighed, but John assured me that he was fine, and back in his box eating happily. I could picture him picking at his hay net as I sat just feet in front of him, worrying about him and smoking cigarettes. As we made our way slowly through the countryside, with the horsebox rattling behind us, John told me what he thought of the way I had raced. In his lovely cor blimey way he said: 'You done well, you really did. You looked good too and there was a point out there where I thought you were going to win it.' That was credit enough for me.

Arriving at Heads Farm, Dancing Marabout walked unsteadily down the ramp of the box and John put him to bed. I headed for the pub with Trigger and his girlfriend, Charlotte, where I got very drunk, very quickly.

I suppose I could have left John and Dancing Marabout and driven back to London with Rose, Jack and Lara but somehow I wanted to make sure that he got back home safely. I could see that Rose and the children were disappointed, but John stepped in, telling them the job wasn't finished until the horse was back in the stable. Although no one said it, I was one of them now.

As we staggered out of the pub, Trigger said he'd see me in the morning but I could have a lie-in and I'd be expected at 8 a.m. to ride second lot. Emotionally charged, I lay down on my bed not really believing what I had done and slept for ten hours. The following morning I rode again. This was my life now and I didn't want to let it go.

EPILOGUE

I rode two horses that morning. It was chilly as we went down to the gallops. All the lads were very polite. John repeated what he had said in the lorry on the way back, that I had done well, better than anyone thought or expected. I don't know if he meant it but it was great to be told it nonetheless. I certainly got the feeling that the lads had a sort of grudging respect for me now, and there were a few handshakes before it was back down to business. After we returned from the gallops, I slid off the back of the last horse I rode that day and I said goodbye to them all. They were my friends now, my equals, and without them I would never have been able to fulfil this dream. I had a bath, got into the car and headed for junction 14 of the M4. Halfway back to London I began to cry. Tears rolled down my cheeks. I was in a quandary, unable to fathom whether they were tears of joy at what I had done, what I had achieved, or tears of sorrow and anger at the life I was leaving behind.

One of the first things I did when I got back into my routine was redecorate my office with photos taken at Towcester of myself and Dancing Marabout. I then dug deep into a chest that I had not opened for more than thirty years. There, under mountains of diaries and letters and invitations, I found a large brown envelope with around thirty black and white photographs from my childhood. They were pictures of me and Nugget and Bracken and numerous other horses and ponies that I had known and loved. I took them out, and started fixing them onto my office wall. I found some handwritten postcards from Sir Mark Prescott depicting racing scenes – they went up, too. It was a new office. No longer festooned with media clippings, awards that I'd won, big stories that I'd written. Some of those stayed but they were now jostling for position with pictures from another life.

At first it was difficult. I'd been away from my family for months. My daily routine was as different as it was possible to be. I was back to getting up at 7.30, packing the children off to school, cycling with Lara and walking Billy the dog. I spoke to Charlie a lot and longingly looked at the pictures on my office wall where my other life had been. I missed it badly but, like the day I first set off in the car for Heads Farm, I knew I'd have to throw myself back into London with a vengeance. It wasn't easy. I found concentration difficult, I was restless and unable to get down to even the simplest chores. But things improved and gradually I got back into a routine. Not a day passed without me thinking of my time at Heads Farm.

And that was very much how it was until April. I spent the winter months working and eating. I worried about my weight at first, and then gradually started to put it back on. From time to time I ate too much, but there was little of the serious gluttony that I had enjoyed so much a year before. The cigarettes went almost immediately although, I am rather ashamed to say, they come back into my life from time to time.

One spring morning in Oxfordshire, where the sun was shining and the birds were singing, we were heading off to the pub for lunch. I'd gone there for a story, one that I wasn't immediately set alight by, but a story nevertheless, and one in which I could accommodate the children – luxury, really, being able to take your children to work. One that would put bread on the table. I had been back in my London media skin for six months. Things were fine but I still had moments – sort of every hour of every day – when I thought I had made a big mistake, when I felt that I should have stayed at Heads Farm and rearranged my life accordingly.

Then the phone rang. It was Charlie asking me to ride in another race. 'This time we've a real chance of winning it. I've got a plan and I've got a horse for you. He's called Freeze the Flame and he's a bloody good horse. Trigger is going to give him a prep race for you a month before your race. What do you reckon?' What did I reckon? It was the best idea I had heard in a long time. I looked around me in the car. 'Dad? Are you going to ride again?' 'Yes, darling. And this time I am going to win.'

* * *

Early one evening at the beginning of May off I go back to Heads Farm for the first time since the autumn. Charlie is away, but Trigger and Albert and John and Nicky and Kirill and Josef are all still ensconced. They are still mucking out stables, patting and cuddling horses and hoping against hope that their charges will run faster and longer than the ones that Charlie chooses to pit them against. Bianca has gone and when I ask why a silence descends. There had been 'an incident', Albert tells me, and Bianca left under a cloud. I knew better than to ask any more.

Charlie has changed his mind about Freeze the Flame. He now wants me to ride the big lolloping horse The Local. 'Locey', as Josef calls him, has won more than £50,000 for Charlie and, although now perhaps past his prime, is sound and strong and, above all, gives me great confidence, and has recently come out of semi-retirement.

This time around I decide I can do the race and the weight by riding out twice a week, not four times. But that is without taking into account the horror show that awaits me at Boots in Wantage. In I go, as I did in the autumn. The same faces are there. The nurses, the teachers, the stable lads and lasses and the pensioners queuing and aching and coughing and sputtering, waiting to collect the pills and potions that will, they hope, patch up their creaking bodies and bruised limbs.

True enough, my trousers are tight and the collar on my shirt doesn't quite do up as snugly as it once did but there is a certain confidence seeping from me as I get onto the weighing scales. As I did in the autumn, I put the ticket in my pocket and return to Heads Farm where I brew a pot of coffee, light a cigarette and unfold the shiny piece of paper that will tell me how far I have to go, what weight I have to lose if I am to have any chance at all of getting round the bends and undulations at Newbury racecourse on 2 July. The news is not good. Fifteen stone and two pounds. That means in six months I have put on three stone. Drastic action will have to be taken.

Every Thursday morning I drive down to Head's Farm. Leaving at 5.15, I get there by 6.30, sometimes earlier. And so it starts again. I eat little, ride two, sometimes three lots, then exhaustion engulfs me. Charlie goes off to the office to placate and soothe owners, to plot and plan and buy and sell the horses in his charge.

One warm morning in late June, with my weight teetering around the 13 stone mark, and exactly a week to go before my second race I go to tack up The Local. I run my hands over the leather and buckles and hear the jangle of the bit as I try to put it into his mouth. I check the heaving at the girth straps to ensure that they are tight enough and the fumbling around with the bridle to make sure straps are in the keepers, and that leather is not cracked or parched. As I had done every day last time I was here, I need to make sure that the horse is comfortable enough for it to perform without the material pinching or rubbing during our morning's workout. It also gives me good time to gauge just how the horse is feeling. I rub his nose and ask him to lower his head so the thick lump of steel that is the bit can be placed in his mouth. Some mornings he stands there and opens his mouth, others I have to insert two fingers into the corner where no teeth grow, in order to cajole and convince him to stretch his jaw. This morning he does it with ease and no fuss. He opens his mouth, a big wide, yawning open that says to me he's feeling good and wants to get on with it.

As the sun rises and a haze hovers over the corn and barley fields we make our way to the gallops. The Local is very perky, ears pricked. We've taken our instructions, as usual, in the yard, and I am to hack up the gallops once. Others around me are cantering, some steady, some fast. Some are going up once, others twice, depending on the fitness of the horse beneath them, when they'd last raced and how long they'd been in work for. The Local had raced recently with the great AP guiding him round, where he only managed sixth. 'He doesn't like McCoy,' somebody shouts from the back of the field when I ask why he only came sixth. 'What about Trigger? Does he like him?' I shout back.

Trigger, who has been with horses all his working life, has never actually ridden in a race. Although he did not acknowledge what role I might have had, not long after I left Heads Farm he decided that he was going to race at the very track at Newbury where I would be making my second outing soon after him.

Not long after I arrived at Newbury, I joined the party as we went off to watch Trigger run his race. Our hopes were high, a feeling in the pit of the stomach that Trigger, a man who has ridden thousands of different horses, would win his first race in public. He was well prepared, had lost weight and was down below 12 stone. He knew exactly how he was going to ride The Local – fast and furious.

Down at the start at Newbury there was a good bit of jostling for position, of waiting around, and then they were off. Trigger did exactly as he said he was going to do, and hit the front immediately. I needed to study what he was doing in order to assess how the horse was going to perform. In two weeks time I would be the jockey, on the same horse over the same distance at the same racetrack. Trigger's effort was going to be my blueprint, only it wasn't. Charging along the back straight for a mile, round the left-hand bend, at several points in the race more than fifteen lengths ahead of all rivals, Trigger was going to do it. The horse was going to win. And then, with five furlongs to run coming into the home straight, The Local just stopped. Trigger had given him a pull to let him fill his lungs, but instead he just dug his toes in and lost all interest in running. Trigger could do nothing but sit there as Mark Weeks, who had been his protégé at Heads Farm, went storming past on a horse that glistened and gleamed and looked superior in every way to every other horse in the race. Trigger came ninth. Although he was sanguine, deep down it was clear that he was quite angry. Tactically he had messed it up, but that was only with hindsight. If he'd stormed off and won he would have been a hero. He hadn't and he wasn't.

*   *   *

West Berkshire is experiencing something of a heatwave with temperatures hitting highs of 80 plus at the end of June. The ground is hard and unyielding and I weigh more than 13 stone – 13 stone 5lb to be precise – just three days before my race at Newbury. It is a disaster. I decide to starve. For forty-eight hours I eat nothing, sip water, drink black coffee, smoke cigarettes and sleep. I remember everything about the year before, and wonder how I had kept it up for so long. Some afternoons I lie down to read a book and wake up three hours later. I ride two horses only in the morning, wrapped in sweaters and a freezer coat, and when I climb down at 9 a.m. the shirt on my back is dripping, soaked with a pungent, metallic sweat that lingers long after the shirt has been dried in the hot sun. I take laxatives and eat diuretic pills and drink a can of Red Bull, remembering the rush at Towcester and the contents of AP McCoy's car.

Counting down to the race, I weigh in at my lightest, at 12 stone 11lb. I have lost eight pounds in twenty-four hours by starving and dehydrating myself, helped by the fact that the temperature in the car is 36 degrees. I know that most of this weight is water so it means that I have to sip it in very small quantities as the race approaches, taking on just enough to sustain the sweat and to salve the burning, dry tongue.

When I get back to Heads Farm, Albert comes to the house to see me. Highland Laddie, a horse in Charlie's charge, had collapsed just over the finishing line at Worcester when coming third. He was exhausted, dehydrated, and just lay there on the track. Racing was held up for over an hour and then the track announced that it had run out of water and the meeting was abandoned after the first race. Water was indeed in short supply.

While I sat in the kitchen picking at a salad and contemplating a swim early in the evening, I thought of Charlie who had dispatched himself to the magic fat clinic in Austria. It is his second visit in as many months. Last time he went he lost ten pounds in a week, came back and put the entire lot back on again in a matter of days. For nearly a year he has sat watching me struggle and starve and run and swim and sauna and try to get fit. He has watched the endless rising trots for mile upon mile, he has eaten the lentils and the salads I have prepared and he has witnessed what can be done. How you can lose weight, live a dream, do something for yourself. He can see the sense of achievement – after all, he enabled me – and when I started on the journey I kept urging him to come with me, to do it, to get back out there and ride those horses. Years ago he used to go with the string down to the gallops on his hack. And then the winners had come thick and fast and he got too fat, and apart from cranky gurus and crazy wizards he won't listen to anyone.

The morning after I go to the house and prepare myself for the task for the last time, I run on the spot for ten minutes and then take a hot, hot bath. I lie in the water with the hot tap running and the sweat oozing from every pore and dripping down my face, off the end of my nose and dripping from my ear lobes. This time, though, I have left it too long and too late. I've not lost the weight I needed to. I'm teetering, a stone overweight.

At noon precisely Trigger, Josef and I leave for Newbury racecourse in the box. The Local is behind us. He's very calm, an old hand. He's been in this box and gone off to the races lots of times before. We talk and smoke a bit; despite it being a place of work, no one minds the smoking. No one cares. It is glorious.

About an hour before the off I go into the weighing room. The silks fit, the breeches slide on easily and I begin to wonder where the extra stone I'm carrying is hiding. The valet has laid out my saddle, bridle and hat for me. I weigh out and the scales creak past the 13 stone mark. I walk out into the sunshine, the crowd is big, out into the parade ring where Trigger, Josef and the Marsdens are waiting to greet me. We have a chat, Trigger gives me my instructions and Janet Marsden says, 'Don't be too hard on him'. For this race I am carrying a stick.

The Local trots nicely in an anticlockwise fashion down towards the start. The starter talks to us and says he is not going to drop his flag until we are all in line. Backwards and forwards we go, jostling for position, and then in a flash the flag goes down. The first half-mile is straight and green and soft. I pull him sharply to the left to try and pick up the inside rail and the jockey behind me screams out, 'Get out of the fucking way, you'll kill us'. I apologize and on we go. A horse roars up on my outside but The Local is still there battling against the three on the inside rail and one on my right. He is making a good job of it. Round the left-hand bend and now we are in the home straight with just half a mile to go. I realize that my stirrups are too long, my legs are seizing and although The Local doesn't stop dead as he did with Trigger, he is slowing down. I tilt forward and shout words of encouragement to him and then a horse, brimming full with energy, storms past me on the right. I pick up my stick and give him two hard slaps on the quarter but there is no response, nothing. Another horse passes me and I know it is the weight. My weight is too much for him.

Had I been a stone lighter I might have won. I'd bettered Trigger's place of two weeks earlier. The opposition was of lesser quality but I had nevertheless raced over the same distance, along the same track, carrying more than one stone overweight. The jockey who won promptly fell off just past the finishing post suffering from exhaustion. I was beaten by eleven lengths. I should have won by at least three. Damn. As it is I come fifth. Elated, exhausted, I weigh out and swiftly sink a pint of Pimm's before heading back to my other life in London.

POSTSCRIPT

On Thursday 1 July 2010, more or less a year after my last race, I went to Newbury for a race meeting. And there was Josef in his shiny suit and shoes, all done up, looking the dog's bollocks. His teeth were still missing. He had a runner in his charge that he was looking after. He saw me and I ran up to him and gave him a great hug. He asked me when I was coming to Heads Farm again, when we would see each other, then he burst into tears and said that Barry and Janet Marsden had given him – yes, just gifted him – The Local. I had never seen anyone, ever in my entire life, as happy as Josef. I told him I loved The Local too and wondered whether he might sell him to me. 'Mr Dominic, not for one million pounds, if you took it out of your pocket now to try to give it to me I would say no. He is mine and I love him.'

That's what horses can do to you.

ACKNOWLEDGEMENTS

For The Horse, and for Rose who, quite unwisely encouraged me to revive my love affair with them.

Writing this book involved a huge amount of teamwork. My thanks goes firstly to the team captain Charlie Egerton without whose co-operation none of it would have been possible, his generosity knows no bounds. A fine, complicated person with a huge heart and spirit and a very good trainer too. Contrary to what Charlie said about not wanting to sell Heads Farm in the autumn of 2010 he did just that, making £12 million befoe moving himself and his horses to Lambourn. Dancing Marabout you made my dream come true. The Local for letting me do it again and for Barry and Janet Marsden his owners. For Trigger, Albert, John and Josef who all held my hand along the way and made sure I didn't end up pulped or in hospital.

Although this idea had been festering in me for many years it took, like many things in my life, a sharp kick to get it going. The kick didn't come from a horse but from my wife Rose. She'll never know how grateful I am as I am always remiss with praise. My children, Jack and Lara too who got so excited by the idea that when asked by school friends and parents 'what does your daddy do?' replied unblinkingly, 'don't you know, he's a famous jockey!' I think in some small way they were proud of me. Not as proud as I am of them though for having endured the endless embarrassment and weeks away from home. Mr McGregor, the gardener at Heads Farm for an endless source of jokes, mimickery and amusement, Lucy Cowans, Carrie, Charlotte, Nicky, Jason, Eldiiar, Kiril and all the unsung heroes – the stable lads at Heads Farm. I hope I have remembered it as it happened and not as I dreamed it.

For Jimmy McCarthy and AP McCoy, who, when I had more or less given up any hope of riding in a race both gave salient advice and huge encouragement. True gladiators the pair. To all at the British Racing School, but particularly Richard Perham for his insight and inspiration. For Ian Bent at the BBC, a fine producer and a friend who was always there with encouragement. Robin Harvie at 4th Estate for not giving up on me. Particular thanks to Philip Beresford who has been a great friend, in many different ways, for many years, ditto Ralph Ward-Jackson. For my neighbour Abdul Majoud who taught me how to run and get fit. Jimmy and Jane George and Martin Mitchell who smoothed my way to the British Racing School. Sir Mark Prescott for invaluable help with the manuscript and much else besides. Valerie Cooper, Diana Cooper, Alan Cooper, Patrick Cooper and Jonathan Cooper who, although not with us, was almost certainly pissing himself with laughter somewhere not too far away when I had my great day. Jonathan's son, also my godson Linus Cooper who I hope catches the horse bug. Bill Oppenheim, a man who brings a much needed intellect to the business of thoroughbred horseracing and breeding. Keith Archer, Danny Rosenbaum, Piers Pottinger, David Stanistreet, Rose & Kevin Hicks and Edward the horse, kinder individuals it would be harder to come across. My mum and my late dad because without them none of this would ever have happened. George and Mouse Campbell and George's brother and of course the one eyed giant, Daz who really got it all going. Everyone who sponsored me. And lastly for everyone out there who has a dream.